When Dad had served his articles period, he was offered a junior partnership on certain financial terms, sufficiently to contemplate marriage if he obtained the right answer and consent of my GrandDad.

Victor Newberg, his boss, was careful with both his money and his praise and was not generous with either. Although not a difficult man, he was hard to please and expected his "pound of flesh" from employees, of which there were three others – an office boy and two clerks - both on Bob Cratchit wages.

CW01498956

Chapter 2

Childhood and Education

I remember when I was only six years old, being in a crocodile of some twelve tots, winding across the deserted Common to the main road on our way to school. We had to pass along a railed pavement by an asylum before crossing the main road to another small Common by the school. We saw hands clasping the tall bars of the railings, pale faces peering curiously at us – the occasional hand waved, or "Hello" spoken, assured us that they were real people. I was still thinking of them when I reached school. I was a quiet boy and I wondered if my Dad said "Hello" to them if he saw them when young, or coming this way to his work. I made a mental note to ask him. When I did so he told me "Never dismiss anyone at face value."

In 1928 I was eight years old and, after going to a Kindergarten in the early days where I had shown some promise and bright physical talents, I had been moved to a much larger church school, St. Leonard's, in Streatham. My Uncle Ron had married my Aunt Lil in St. Leonard's Church. I had been christened there also.

Our home was a modest terraced house, quite near shops and Commons, of which there were several. My way home from school was either via private sanded roads with superior properties, or else down through the local shops via the tramway route. I mostly chose the quiet way as I rather enjoyed the crunchy feel of the road under my feet, especially when run-

The three brothers: Kenneth, Douglas and Gordon.
Taken approximately 1930.

ning. I was fleet of foot and enjoyed the bracing feeling I got in hurrying everywhere. I felt that I was being carried along by the wind when running along the pavements, and therefore rarely lingered, except when passing the few shops when I took the quickest way home. In the winter, as it got dark when I left school on a lot of evenings, I felt safer with the comfort of the streetlights and shop windows.

One dusky evening I was going home past the shops, and the lights were all on. I started staring in the gloriously glamorous illuminated windows and saw a luscious display of sweets and chocolates. I was hungry and noted that no one was in the shop. I timidly entered. Then I impulsively grabbed the nearest delicious looking chocolate bar and started running away.

"Hey, young man" said a voice in front of me "You won't be very happy with eating cardboard! That'll teach you a lesson! Ha! Ha! Ha!" said the proprietor in my ears. The lesson helped me for the rest of my life!

Meanwhile my Dad's boss, Mr Newberg, had died and so Dad had to look for his next career move. First of all he had bought a house being built in a respectable part of Wallington (not the best, of course, but what his budget allowed and with a lamppost outside.) This last point was very important to my careful Dad, for security purposes, as he was conscious of "foot-pads" (thieving opportunists) as he called them! It turned out to be true also….

In moving to this house I had to go to a secondary school and there I took my entry exam for Wallington Grammar School. That period, though not long, was not too happy… first I was <u>new</u>, second I had abominably curly hair and lastly they considered I spoke "posh"!! The school captain told me they were not picking me for the school football teams as I had been so boastful about my prowess! In other words, I was a big-head.

However that was a useful period for me for the experience it gave. I was not interested in <u>girls</u>. In line with the attitude of most boys my age in those days, I thought girls were silly. But the school captain's girl pestered me in the parks, etc. and I suppose she inadvertently kept me out of his team!

Whilst at this school I found out about the presence of bullying, but I was not there for long as the term ended in August and in September I was to go to the Grammar School. I spent all possible time in the outdoors playing soccer and cricket in the parks around the area, which were several, plus some lovely countryside for exploration! I came across plenty of excitement in contesting with various local boys and even gangs. There were caves around an old brick factory, a sandpit of some size plus streams and ponds. It was a sort of heaven with a few snags thrown in! Lovely! Being a fast runner helped me a lot in getting out of awkward spots of bother. As I was small and athletic, it often meant getting home undamaged. My Mother was a great support to us boys! She didn't make a fuss. My brother, Ken, was fond of teasing and jeering at the wrong sort of chaps and often needed rescuing! He was three years younger than me, and a brilliant cricketer, especially when he was older.

The Grammar School was once the Girls' School of the same order, but they had built a brand new one quite nearby. We boys were shifted into the old Girls' school whilst a new one for us was being built. Ours was down in a very useful setting for sports fields with plenty of land and on a main road between Croydon and Sutton.

We were rather crowded for two years but it was adequate as we had two "remove" forms to reduce clashing between forms, i.e. we reduced the number of forms in the school temporarily. The class sizes consisted of around twenty-eight to thirty pupils each. My adolescent years were spent there until "Matric" time for me and I left in 1936.

Grammar School was a great change for me and I was put in 2A at the age of nine with all the rest of the class a year older – again providing an opportunity to meet a bully or two. This time I knew more and coped rather better. On the study side, they had made an error so in 1930 I was held back for a year. A lot of the work was repeated, but I had better masters and so did pretty well all round! It was still a "rugger" school and I was still small (nicknamed Minnie) and rugby simply wasn't my game. Eventually I started a soccer team outside the school and, even though we were a rugger school and not a soccer one, the Headmaster reluctantly permitted us to wear our school badge on a white shirt. This made us look like "Wallington Spurs"! He was not a man for sport actually, but a brilliant man on English. He formed a little group of boys good at English and called it "the Makyrs" and I was privileged to be asked to join. It may have helped about the soccer. Okay!

It was whilst I was in my first year in 2A that I earned the label "Minnie". It was because a boy called Lambert, who "ragged" me a bit, got 100 lines for some folly from the excellent French master, Mr Britton. I laughed "Ha! Ha!" and got 200 lines!

They were to be written after school hours in the classroom, of course, alongside Lambert.... Another lesson learnt in life, eh? Later, during wartime, the "Brittons" moved to a house opposite 23 Crichton Avenue and became close friends of my parents. Mr Britton was the reason I became interested in foreign languages in general. He was strict but first class.

Now, back to the soccer. It wasn't easy to get fixtures, but I got one or two to play against my previous school, Bandon Hill Secondary. They were played in either Beddington Park or a smaller park next to St Mary's Church (called the Paddock!). Each park had goal posts as a special treat. One other park, the Recreation Ground, also was suitable but hard to book. Our opponents were selected by Mr Southern, a master at Bandon Hill School, who also managed Surrey Boys team, rather hot stuff! He was a great help to me. Other fixtures were matches against rugger boys from my own school when I could wangle it!

Sometimes I had to summon a team to be opponents, and that was some job! But the boys from poorer homes knew their stuff all right and we had worthwhile mixed games often. My younger brother Ken often played for us and he was quite a star!

Chapter 3:

Working Matters

Whilst enjoying the soccer in my remaining days at school, a letter came round telling of a job on offer from the Prudential Assurance Company. My ears pricked up. I knew of it as a company because my young and very attractive Aunt Hilda once had had a fiancé who was in that company, and he had spoken well of it. Her engagement did not last; she had loads of boyfriends (or young men I should say) in her time and used me as a chaperon, something necessary in those days! I found it to be a most intriguing experience, and learnt better manners, more expressive conversation, and a feeling of being more into the adult world! Moreover, my aunt was a talented dancer and singer – a striking personality indeed!

Anyway I went for an interview in their Sutton office and two others from my form were there for it also. I got the job – I think because I was prepared to go to their Guildford office if required to do so – and hooray! I was in business…. the Guildford question was a ploy no doubt! The pay was £50 a year, or £1 a week in fact. My mother asked for seven shillings a week to help with the finance, and I was left with the grand sum of seven shillings for myself after stoppages! Wow! Anyway I hadn't missed the chance – jobs were hard to get. I was the first chap to get a job from school that year.

I was nervous that first day at the office, as an office boy, making the tea for three other seniors including the manager. I had a jerky start, largely due to the chap immediately above me (Ritz by name) who delighted in ridiculing me, but also insinuating enough opinions about the chief clerk, a gentle man of modest ambitions to get secretive chuckles from the 2nd clerk and hidden smiles from me. Ritz had a favourite song which he used to sing about the chief clerk, George Formby's "You'd be far better off in a home!" After a year or so of this, I eventually had a fight with him and he got the worst of it! I was playing regularly for "the Pru" at soccer and cricket and I had kept my fitness as a result of it. And I had grown a bit too.

We'd had a summer holiday in Clacton-on-Sea just before and Dad and I got to know each other's views for the future during those two weeks. He actually asked me what I thought he should do about his prospects, now that Newberg had died. Was he to take the chance to take over? Or, go to George Kents (one of their big accounts) as that firm's only accountant? I said, greatly flattered, "Go ahead, Dad! Take over!!" But he chose the latter. He had a great friendship with most of their staff in London and they greatly required him. It was in character with his gentle nature and caution to make this decision. But Mother and I thought he could cope with Newberg & Co – they had great clients (among them Brooklands Racetrack & Oppenheimers of medical fame) as well as George Kent & Co!

My life at the Sutton office and at home in this period was largely sport plus working hard, as the Pru got their money's worth, and I also fitted in some tennis up at Wallington Cricket and Tennis Club – it was very convenient. I had, as a schoolboy, complemented my pocket money as a scorer for this cricket club on Saturdays and the Croydon CC on Sundays when required. Good money plus tea thrown in! So you see, I kept busy and earning where possible…. In the case of the tennis club I had my best pal Roy as a partner and we met a circle of other friends there, amongst whom two who became business associates in later times.

Back to the Pru – I sometimes had found that the office routine was rather monotonous, but the sport side eventually found a gap for me. I had played for Ibis Football & Cricket Club (the Pru's club) and quickly seemed to get known quite well there.

Someone told me of a chance to get involved in a wider side of the firm and so I applied for a move to the Whitechapel branch – and got it! A little more salary included in the position covered the extra expenses involved in travelling, so it suited very well indeed. Rather than being just a clerk in an office, I was joining a divisional office which had a wider scope for promotion and subjects as the future could prove.

Chapter 4:
Sign Up and Love Blossoms

T he country was getting a little closer to the big event of war and so in 1938 I joined the Territorials at Balham Barracks of the Royal Signal Corps – as did many men of my age at the time. In my school Class V of thirty-one pupils, eight joined up that week – three of them where I went. So I had companions in a completely new aspect of life. And my goodness it did take me by surprise….. firstly, I hadn't been shown how to dress with the gear supplied. It was riding kit… and my attempt was greeted with ribald laughs all round! Putties all over the place! (They were the strips of khaki we had to wear as leggings). However, that was a detail. Secondly, the discipline was very tough, and we were treated just as the cinema films demonstrate – as nit-wits, which of course we were…..

Very soon the annual camp came (July 1938) and we were putting up our tents. Very early rising with an outdoor disciplined breakfast followed by drill for an hour and so on, made a non-stop day. However, we didn't know what was to come, which, when it did, put an end to the whole thing. We were washed out by extremely heavy and perpetual rainfall and had to go home early, damp and contrite, to <u>Mother</u>! Incidentally, territorial troops didn't get paid the nominal amount of two shillings a day, except at camp or war, so we didn't make much out of that! Soon I got into learning the Morse code, wireless operation, and sema-phore on a twice an evening a week basis and I found it very

Gordon Huntington, aged 18.

intriguing. I achieved a high grading when the results came out. I was astounded by the lack of equipment, but not the discipline.

When war was declared in September 1939, it was to change all our lives. But before it happened, in the preceding year, I had met someone who made another change for me, personally.

During the period of my new job with the Pru I made several friends – my best pal Roy was one of them and two chaps, both called John, whom I'd met at cricket and tennis clubs and who lived locally. With the two Johns I played pontoon, poker and snooker, as well as playing tennis with my friend Roy in opposition to them in the doubles at Wallington CC. We made a very good four and lots of banter went on!

One afternoon, though, we decided to go to a local fair and play skittles etc. It was a pretty popular fair and the attendance was large. We ran out of money quite early on at the sideshows and one John said, "Let's look for girls!! That'll be cheap enough." "Do any of us know any?" Well none of us did – we had been too busy in other directions to give any thought to that department.

Anyway we gathered round a sideshow and there were three girls together around the same one, all in Wallington's Girls Grammar School uniform. John H deliberately barged into one of them and she yelped but took it very well, so we got moving round the show with them for the rest of the afternoon and said we would see them home. I knew that one of them, Edna Clark, lived quite near to me, but two of the girls departed to go to their nearby homes. The two Johns and I were left to finish off the politeness to see her home. I had little to say and seemed to be walking in the gutter most of the time, whilst the other two appeared to be making inane remarks quite successfully without me! I had listened however and heard that Edna's mother was not very well. When we departed happily I had an idea!.....

I made haste to a little more money that I had saved and bought a small posy of flowers, took it round to Edna's house about half a mile away and presented it to her for her mother with a certain panache. "Hope your mother gets better soon!" Edna looked pleasantly surprised and smiled back. What a pretty girl too. "Might see you again soon?" "You never know" she replied "Goodbye."

The following week I rang her number and she answered. "Would you come to the pictures with me?" "Yes" she said, "be delighted". "When?" "How's about Friday?" she said (showing off). "Okay, fine." And that was that.....

The remaining days till then were a delightful daze and inclined to put me off guard at the office. Ritz had several attempts at bringing me into a bantering discussion or two but I was a damp squib as far as that went.

We went to the Granada Sutton – a new cinema near the office, and I was rather nervous to start with but Edna seemed fully in control. It was my first date ever and I didn't have a sister so it was almost like being with a beautiful someone from another planet.

However a few jocular comments did not seem to go down too badly. I can't remember what we saw but, in those days, there was usually one main film plus a cartoon and a stage show, of short duration, for one's money. The latter part, on this occasion, had a stuttering comedian who made me feel uncomfortable because my family upbringing taught me never to mock the less fortunate.

To my great pleasure Edna, who must have sensed my disapproval, whispered "Hello! Hello! I don't approve either." We had a very good journey home after that and I saw her to her door with my spirits very high! She was very pretty, and neat in her general appearance and manner. I particularly admired the way she walked!

When telling my parents of this auspicious love incident of my life and mentioning Edna Clark, my mother said "One of the Clark sisters?" I said "Yes – but only one sister, Mother!" I was informed that my parents knew Mrs Clark very well. They

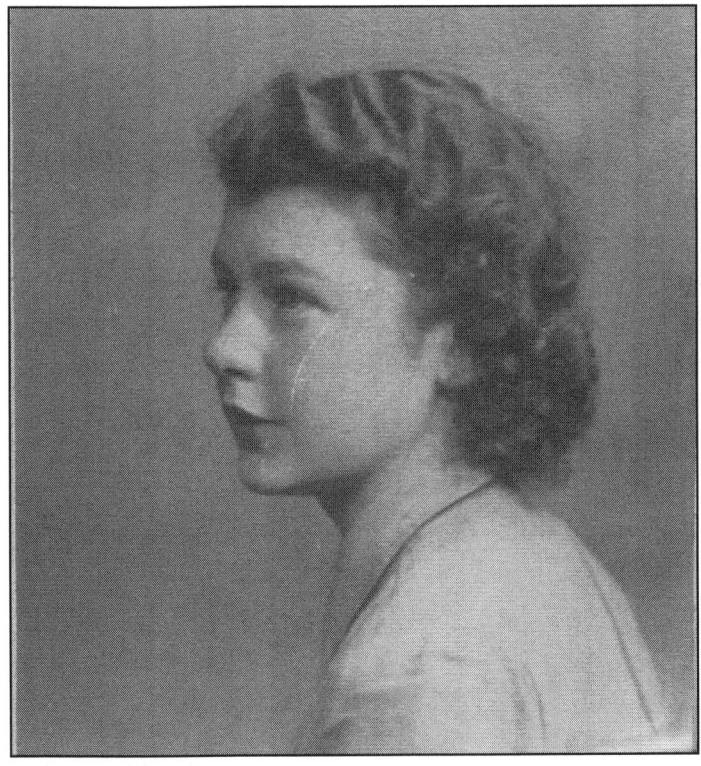

D. Edna Huntington, taken approximately
1935.

played cards with her a good deal at the Bowling Club where they were members and I was told what a very nice person she was and a widow at that!

Anyway they approved.... Mrs Clark had another daughter, Marjorie. Marjorie was the elder and worked at I.C.I., a large company in London. I wasn't quite sure whether it was a good thing that they knew all this – but there you go!

So from then on we dated when we could until the war started in September 1939. Edna got a job with the National Provincial Bank in Croydon as a machinist (teller) and I got settled in with the Prudential at Whitechapel. One incident I do recall is about my interest in horse racing. I had always seemed rather receptive in intuition over matters like chess, bridge and racing. I was never foolish to ignore the risks involved in the latter, but I did like to sport a shilling (or even sixpence) here and there and therefore kept in touch with what went on wherever possible. I got into the way of checking via the press, at work, by nipping down to the newsvendor just outside our office and finding out certain results. Not too often, as I could be seen going out by the public part of the building from our department upstairs. I was called into the District Manager's office one day. The boss said, "What's going to win the 3 o'clock today, Huntington, do you think?" Taken aback I said, "I don't know, sir". "Oh, do you think your Dad would like your being interested at all?" "No, sir." "Well, nor do I. I don't think it's at all good for you, so that makes two of us, doesn't it?" "Yes, sir." "Well you bear it in mind, laddie, and go back to your work. We are pleased with you so far. Go on!"

Chapter 5

The Call Up – September 1939

W e had been called up a few days before any real action occurred and all of us will never forget the first time the air raid warning sirens went off almost immediately after war had been declared – the big day when they tested them without telling us! It was a trial and they were assessing our reactions! We were stationed in Queensgate and we were ordered downstairs to the floor below and packed in like sardines, officers and men, without any ado. After an hour or so of this, the "all clear" was sounded and we all got sorted out to receive some news from the RSM (Regimental Sergeant Major) to clarify matters. This included dividing us into our trades i.e. wireless operators, linesmen, electricians and clerical staff. Then we had drill in Sections Centre as a daily item plus lectures on the work to be done by the regiment, 1st London Divisional Signals by name. After a few days of this, certain of us were returned to barracks for training in our particular groups. This meant perfecting the Morse code and other forms of signalling, plus drill, etc. I very much enjoyed this and the allotting of "billets" nearby for sleeping. I was lucky to get quite a respectable house with pleasant owners.

The training was quite hectic – it appeared that operators were required to think again instead of just being ordered about! The discipline was good and we were now getting two shillings a day – hooray! I began to make friends with the other operators and office staff.

Gordon Harold Huntington, Royal Signals
(then 2ⁿᵈ Queens), 1938.
Photograph with hand written message,
"To Edna with all my love, Gordon".

The Prudential were going to pay me my £70 a year through my modest bank account, so I was better off than a lot of them. I was going to keep very quiet about that as I soon found that there were plenty of short-term borrowers about. I gained prestige when I had a "hassle" with quite a tough chap. He was a linesman who thought I was a "tart" and with whom I was placed for a while in a corrugated iron shed in a corner of the barracks. We had another companion called Hatchett who had a job in an office somewhere before the war came. The linesman and I made such a noise in the metal box that it drew attention to us. When we went on parade I was asked about it, and my bruised elbow. How did I get it? "Well, I fell over, sir" I said "coming to this parade." "Just you watch it, then" said the RSM. "Yes, sir." I began to make a few friends then and it helped to pass any spare time there until the next move. Edna and I kept in touch frequently by letter and telephone in the quiet period and we became strong friends.

As I said before, reputations grow quickly and my little group was based largely on physically very fit people who were interested in sport, chess and snooker and this continued through to the next place where we were to be stationed – Eastbourne! As my knowledge of communication had grown, I was singled out for a small advance party to prepare the way, although none of us knew it until the last moment, of course! Secrecy had become the 1939 rule of law, and quite right too. The man in charge was a Major and quickly he turned out to be very good to have in charge. We worked, ate and slept in a house near the sea at the Beachy Head end of Eastbourne – quite a select area. More often than not, I was put on a large switchboard with contacts to goodness knows whom! I enjoyed that very much and listened in to mostly military items etc. – but there were the most interesting ones sometimes, giving me a good idea how some of the officers behaved with the ladies?!

The rest of our regiment came down in a week or two and we were then put into billets according to our trades and units. I got an early choice with a room overlooking the sea! From that time on we operated as a complete unit for meals, drill and training. Our section was D Section (or DON). I continued with my shift work at the big house on the switchboard – one night shift every other night and so on with the day shift the same. I found soon that it turned out to be very convenient for a quick visit home. The winter was to be a hard one and some of us began to feel out of sorts, and I was one of several to catch a cold. We went to the Medical Officer and he turned out to be a man who had played for England at rugby. He gave about twelve of us leave for seven days, after a day or two in barracks. Surprise, surprise!

I was regularly in touch with Edna by letter and she asked me to go to Edinburgh if I could. At least her mother asked me! They were both staying at her aunt's house for a while and her aunt was away in Canada! I naturally said, "Yes" and got a railway warrant to help me. What a break! I left right away and Edna met me at the station the next day. We did everything we could for the next few days and I kissed her for the first time by Scot's Monument in Princes Street up there after a delicious coffee in one of the many restaurants (Peak Frean, I think). It was a lovely break and no signs of war at all. We got to know each other very well and I began to think quite seriously about us. I made an arrangement with my mother for her to take Edna to buy a ring. I was an engaged man!

Chapter 6

Action Begins - 1940

An amusing incident occurred during this period, concerning Bella Clark, Edna's mother (née Henderson). She had a great sense of humour and a frequent twinkle in her eye betrayed it. I had managed to get home for a brief stay and whilst there stayed the night at the Clark's place. During the evening there was quite a big air raid and we all decided to go down to the shelter. There was just room for the three of us. The bombing went on and on and we chatted away, quite accustomed to such goings-on. I felt a hand reach into mine and I, of course, squeezed it happily several times and continued to do so. I put my torch on eventually and found it was not Edna's hand but her mother's! She gave her wicked chuckle and then we all laughed. Bella loved that sort of thing. She was a shrewd, joyful person. Her husband, Percy, had died at forty two with kidney troubles and she had brought up the two girls on her own, when Edna was six and her sister, Marjorie, sixteen. Bella was very artistic, a good dressmaker and painter of oils, and had a talent for carving tabletops. I have one of her paintings still and some of my children have her oils in their houses. She played a good hand at cards, including bridge. Many years later, she was to be a great help to Edna when she took a flat in our house at Sydenham to help mind our children. Marjorie, who had married and gone to the Far East with her husband, eventually came back after he was killed in the war there. She had remarried later and brought her second husband back from Canada to England to settle in Sussex, just after the war had ended in 1945.

At this time I actually volunteered to go to Norway with the army but was refused, on medical grounds because I was short sighted. However, very shortly after that the Commanding Officer told the whole unit that we were to stand by for the next move, but didn't say where we were destined to go. I had learnt to drive with an army van, meanwhile, and in the process of training was given charge of a wireless truck– no doubt in case such a situation occurred. Anyway our next base turned out to be near to Ashford, Kent.

I had a great deal of fun with friends in between training and shift duty on the large telephone exchange (it turned out to be a Divisional one in the early stages).

Upon arrival I was one of a small team again to take charge of a large operator's switchboard, once more on a shift basis. It was in a substantial mansion in extensive grounds and that was to be the Divisional HQ. We were all under tentage, when we had erected them, and our team was allocated one with a Lance Corporal in charge. Meals were taken in a roomy tent nearby. It was suddenly all very different, including the food. We had to be regarded now as being in action! The atmosphere became more urgent as we were in an invasion area. Things changed from now on! From that moment, I felt we were really in a war.

The Divisional HQ where we carried out our duties incorporated a lake and a boathouse so we were looking at prosperity all round us. The village was Boughton Lees which included a pub and not much else. My shift work was continued but with added training, including driving a wireless van, to make a break here and there. We were selected for rifle work, including visiting a rifle range near the coast of Kent. The first one was hilarious to look back on but perhaps not at the time! I have never been able to get my ankles flat to the ground whilst lying on the ground and the RSM seized on this. "'Untinon'!" he bellowed, "get those 'eels down!" And he trod on them. No good. "It'll 'arm your shootin', so watch it!"

I had never shot before, and this was live ammunition. In all events, out of the remaining five shots allowed, I had four bulls and one "outer". I think that was an important event in my service life. Soon after I was given one stripe – a Lance Corporal indeed! I was sent on a week's course for military arms knowledge, and got a very good report as well as valuable information for the future. My next post was to the Sevenoaks area where I had my own little squad! Briefly of course, as I soon went back to Boughton Lees, needed on operating duties. Things had become so busy, with the Battle of Britain in full swing above us, and heavy bombing raids were frequent.

One night on duty at the switchboard, I got my stripe taken away as I had left a note on the door saying, "Back soon". I only had a call to make to the 'loo! Well, just my luck, I thought! Quite justified, though.

I was supplied with a wireless van and posted to be attached to the London Irish Rifle Regiment of our Division at Hyde Barracks, under the command of Colonel McNamara. They had their own signals unit, but I liaised with Divisional HQ. I found them very agreeable and friendly and they asked me to play for them at football! A great compliment indeed. We didn't win but I made more friends. I also played for our own unit when they had a match and used my van to get there, which wasn't a long journey. You will be thinking "What a war?"

The role of our unit was, of course, communication all told, and despite there not being a lot of work for the other sections, linesmen and other trades, there were a great deal of electricians to cope with and transport to attend to.

We operators were annoyingly often referred to as "NAAFI tarts" to which we naturally didn't take too kindly, and sometimes caused a "bust up", but by and large the atmosphere of the regiment was very good indeed and brings back very fond memories. Once when I had to go to the kitchen to peel potatoes, I gave a few words of reply to such a taunt from one of the cooks. He waved a meat knife under my nose and I thumped him one in a friendly way. The fuss caused us to be called up before the Company Commander for a strong reprimand, but afterwards the chap threatened me with dire retribution of some sort.

Somewhat later, off duty, I was larking about with a friend of some size compared to me, and I got him in a tied-up mess at wrestling, on his stomach with his legs crossed behind him. (He was Tom Disher whose aunt wrote the "Just William" books, using him as the model for the famous naughty boy!) Anyway, it did so happen that my hatchet man was in a crowd watching it all the time, so I didn't get anything but pleasant contact with the kitchen staff in future! In fact it proved to help me later, indirectly, for my early morning arrivals for duty.

The food in general was good but rationed and rather repetitive. We had tables of eight and No 8 collected it, or whoever was the last arrival. With a good NAAFI canteen we were well provided for, if we had the money to pay for it.

Before being transferred to the London Irish as a clerk, I had quite a number of episodes. There had not been a lot of action for me at Hythe but at Boughton Lees I had been on guard duty and my shift was 2 am to 4 am and all was quiet. I seemed to fall into a dreamy stupor and woke up with a yell when my shoulder was tapped. It was, however, my relief coming for his shift. I felt such an idiot!

Our shifts on that duty and most others were two hours on and four hours off. Another time, a lorry came to the HQ and I asked for a lift, although we were confined to barracks officially. I had noticed the RSM quite near the gate before leaving, so once out of the camp, I asked the driver to let me get off, which he did readily. Once I was back in the camp again I deliberately made my presence known near the office. A voice called out, "'Untinan'". "Yes, sir?" "Didn't I see you in that there vehicle not long ago?" "Yes, sir." "Where were you going then?" "I changed my mind, sir." "Good for you, wasn't it?"

Shortly after that, with a great deal of secrecy, I was moved with the London Irish to Haverhill, Essex. The move up there was a tedious one but I enjoyed driving my own wireless van and following the others. I also had my own room above a shop in the High Street when I arrived!

I was made very welcome by this unit, especially by Colonel McNamara himself who made his rounds quite regularly and seemed 100% in touch with his regiment. The divisional move meant that I had gone with him from Hyde Barracks to Haverhill. I heard he had been a JP (Justice of the Peace) in Chelmsford before the war. He wanted to know details of my wireless equipment and likes and dislikes. I had been asked, as I mentioned before, to play football with them – with the help of their Signals Officer – and I readily complied.

My life became quite fun as the village was a lively one with social occasions, dances, etc. The troops were looked after and made very welcome.

We had exercises and schemes quite often and I was asked to speak to the Signals Section on one occasion about the operating required in our unit – and obliged – I hope not too volubly! After a while I felt very much at home there.

We had one big exercise which affected my future in the war. The occasion was a Divisional one and the London Irish had been appointed as the enemy. Colonel McNamara kept me close to him all the time near the wireless van. He checked up on my map reading to see how the land lay! He said, "Huntington?" "Yes, sir." "Can you find our opponents on the air if I need?" "I should think so, sir." "Then will you do so, please?" "Yes, sir." And I got other voices after a little while. "There you are, sir." And we listened for a while.

"I want you to give them this message when I tell you." "Yes, sir." When the time came I told them that the rendezvous had been changed to "blah blah blah" and to proceed at once. Well that was okay. Back to bed! But I'm afraid to say that we entirely ruined the exercise, as far as they were concerned, by giving victory to the enemy. We won the "war" and captured the home team!!

As a result, I was recalled to my own regiment at once, rather bewildered. They were about twenty-five miles further southeast near a village called Shalford. It seemed to be very busy getting everyone fit. Drills, PT, and a cross-country run which was not the most popular item. I had had plenty of that at school so I enjoyed it and came second over four miles.

I wasn't to be there, though, for very long however......

Chapter 7:

Thoughts pre-Abroad

I sometimes peruse deeply on war, particularly on the worst war, the Great War of 1914-18, which cost millions of young lives, a great many of whom were extremely well disciplined in life already – in middle class families, true to Great Britain and the flag! It was a bloody war too….. My Dad was in it as a Royal Engineer (nowadays Signals) as I was initially. He survived, did not go to France, but remained in England 1917-18. My Uncle Bert Pollock was almost blinded at Gallipoli. Another one, Uncle Ron Huntington, was badly wounded in France and remained scarred for life. He was always very cheerful and I thought he was a scream! He had a happy family and was my Dad's best pal. We had in the house a great batch of magazines all dealing with activities throughout the war, so I was able to become well informed on a lot that happened then.

When I was a youngster, model soldiers were the craze for children with the Germans (Jerry) the enemy. I had two brothers but only Ken had been born then and he was four or five. We made paper pellets and used rubber bands to flick them at lined-up lead soldiers, having decided who was "enemy". Yes it was war all right!

So, including my other brother Douglas (1927 is his birth year), by the time the 1939 war came, we were well briefed on war, very nationalised in our beliefs and knew about enemies, etc. Who was the enemy? Guess? GERMANY!! Of course. I hasten to assure the reader, if any turn up, that I don't bear malice now – I didn't after World War II either.

Children in recent times have probably no information available that gives them any knowledge of what actually goes on in wars, as there may be no relatives who can tell them about wars, or want to. There is now "war" and strong national feeling about sports and any other forms of competition. At school in my time, at least one third of forms 5 and 6 volunteered for the Territorial Army 1938/9 as well as myself. If one has never had a difficult time in one's life it is hard to tackle many problems later. In my case I was quite a different person afterwards with realistic views gained through hard experience. Nowadays, most war films are very often grossly exaggerated and are available for anyone to see. History, in any case, has been relegated mostly in school programmes, even omitted. More's the pity!

This piece of homework below, I think, aptly describes my point of view in this story.

The Bayonet Charge

Grimly, I placed the bayonet over the barrel of the clumsy rifle.
My hands were sweating.
My brain was full of the thought of death, or maybe his petrified face
If I was successful.

Quickly, I charged through the smoke and showers of bullets
At Who?
I did not know,
I had never met him before in my life.

My body tensed up and I let out a terrible groan.
For what?
For fear, for anger or maybe for glory.
I didn't know,
I just obeyed my orders.

Robert Huntington 3G
1969 Age 13
Prince Henry's Grammar School, Evesham

Chapter 8:

On the Move – Essex, Africa and Beyond

In the Divisional HQ near Essex I was summoned to the Adjutant and informed that I was being sent to Catterick, which was HQ Signals and would be in charge of three other men. I found this prospect extremely exciting! It was a surprise to me and of course no reason was given except that it was a request for more skilled operators to be sent into action. I heard later that Colonel McNamara had been posted abroad also. It may have been our less than brilliant result in the recent exercise that had inspired those in the higher ranks above to greater efforts to win the war, one might think. I began to get quite excited with the prospect! So the four of us went by rail to Catterick, HQ for the Royal Signals and quite a way away.

Having got there and reported correctly, I was to join quite a large group, and we were checked over for our records and interviewed separately. Then we were divided into smaller groups of about twelve with one NCO (Non Commissioned Officer) in charge of each. It was divulged that we were going abroad to an unspecified area and we were issued with overseas kit with strange hats, then left to think about it.

There was a rather young officer in charge who was obviously a bit "green" so there were a few winks and furtive jibes around the place. He turned out to be very pleasant and helpful, as we found when we were aboard ship a week later.

I cannot recall the name of the ship but it seemed very comfortable when we found quarters. I was put in a cabin for four, which was great! A lot of instructions were given out – meal times, parade times, ship's details and layout and we were warned about sea-sickness, especially not to eat too much to start with! I don't to this day know why they gave these men the idea of it. When we did set sail and get moving it seemed very smooth to travel in this ship! Yet at breakfast next morning, I was one of very, very few men who attended out of hundreds. After a few days things got more normal and the chaps had found their appetites and, no doubt, balance!

In my plentiful spare time I discreetly explored the ship, including the kitchen. I made friends with an Indian kitchen hand who was carrying a big urn of tea. He offered me a cup and it was lovely. It gave me an idea. I said, "Can you sell me one urn?" He paused and said, "What for, sir?" I said, "To sell cups to my friends who don't get up early." He said, "One shilling." I said, "Thanks." He said, "Any day." So I started a small business next day! I sold an urn full and got two shillings at 1d a cup! So I carried on – and the journey was three weeks to Durban. I got a helper or two and then charged 2d. I became quite rich from that which set me up for the races later in Durban where we were to stay for three weeks.

After that we were put on a different ship (Ile de France) going up to the Suez Canal area. Incidentally, we, apparently, went almost to the South American coast, to avoid submarines, and back to the West African coast, then down round the Cape!

Soon after arriving at our quarters in Durban, we were told that many families had offered to accommodate one of us each for a week's break. It was a nice gesture and I took advantage of it. It turned out to be a comfortably off family with two daughters of twenty and eighteen. They also had a beach house and I was very fortunate: they took me there twice and in lovely weather, plus a run to Johannesburg which was a long journey, full of interest. They were attractive girls and rather flirty. But I was a newly engaged man – on the last day before leaving England. And my mother had agreed to go with Edna to choose a ring! So I was rather guarded towards any advances which did not seem to please them! However, we had lots of laughs and it was a lovely break.

Back in Durban again, I heard that there was a convenient racetrack with a meeting imminent. So, armed with some "tea money", I went along with a pal to try my luck. I noticed that a certain Arab-like chap seemed to be chatting to jockeys on the way to the start and tackled him about local advice. He seemed pleased and said he would help me if possible. He did – twice - and both won! So I gave him evidence of my gratitude for adding to my ill-gotten gains!

At this meeting, a Mexican soldier called Max had chatted to me also and later came up and asked if I would like to be shown around the town. So I said, "Ok!" He said, "I'll bring my knife, Gordon, so you'll be ok", which made me suspicious. We tried a salubrious-looking club with some sort of gambling on offer. I was not too keen on that, but Max was and he got embroiled in cross words over some difference he had with the proprietor on the fairness of the wheel. He produced his vicious-looking knife. "Come on, Max, let's go! Now!" We left in a great hurry. Shortly after that day, we embarked on the "Ile de France" to join the Royal Scots Highlanders for further trouble. However, youth is often oblivious to danger, is it not?

Well, the French liner was one of the finest ships ever made and was popular particularly with the wealthy elite, before this lot began. Now it filled itself with hundreds of troops having done a marvellous job as a troop carrier in the far away waters of the Atlantic and Pacific seas. It was roomy and lush to a degree and I shared a cabin for four in a convenient area for observation of the whole ship.

It seemed to be chock-full of Scottish wee laddies and they made a great deal of noise, especially at meals. They did not seem to like the food much and were generally critical! We got on alright with them and they liked a game of cards and things like that. So I joined in here and there. The trouble was that Scottish packs of cards seemed to have more than four Aces and Kings and a couple or so of Jokers just for fun! So I took my own pack and it paid off on "pontoon"; the "Tommies" derivation of that comes from the French "vingt et un" (21) but nowadays has various names. I started a "Crown and Anchor" game but was raided eventually by a group or two of Scots lads and their plans put my capital situation into some jeopardy, so I gave up and stuck to bridge.

Outside, meanwhile, there were troubles brewing about food, etc., and the Scots wanted to go on strike about it and made a lot of noise with a certain amiable violence as well.

We docked, fortunately, in two days and at Port Taufiq, this side of the Suez Canal and Suez, thence to Cairo. Very hot!!

I don't know what transpired from the mild rioting but those Scots certainly "did their stuff" later in the desert. I missed them – they were so intense – full of "oomph" and fun! Of course, I would go on to marry one! Wouldn't I? Watch out, Untinton!

Not a lot went on for me in Cairo, except, having seen the value of cash and its uses, I mailed my Dad for £10 more and it arrived before the next move. I was able to write some letters to Edna and my parents.

Being an avid reader of Edgar Wallace and HG Wells, I was always interested in mystery. Therefore, before I left, I had fixed a code for writing to Edna. It started with the word "JANE" as a key and spelt the place (like DURBAN), letter by letter after it counting out from 6, 7, 8 and onward until achieved. Thank goodness I didn't have to put NIJNI NOVGROD down! JANE was a cartoon character I admired in the Daily Express cartoons. I learnt later it did work, as Edna asked my Dad to help to decipher it! So, therefore, they did know that I was in Cairo and later on, Tobruk – after all not a bad code! To my knowledge, none of my fellow soldiers practiced such deception. I would have been in awfully hot water, had I been found out! I sometimes mentioned Jane in my letters without putting in a code, just to fool anyone who might suspect my subterfuge!

Here is an example of the code from one of my letters home:

*"Jane **t**old me **of** her li**b**eral inc**r**ement. I tr**u**st she will **k**eep on the straight and narrow! Give her my love too…"*

1st letter after Jane = T (**t**old)
6th letter after T = O (**o**f)
7th letter after O = B (li**b**eral)
8th letter after B = R (inc**r**ement)
9th letter after R = U (tr**u**st)
10th letter after U = K (**k**eep)

I was telling them I was in **TOBRUK!**

I did explore Cairo and visited Alexandra one day in that short time until my friend, George Wheeler, and I were told we were going to Tobruk. Very exciting.

I had played bridge with George on board the first ship and he was good company. It was to be a very long and arduous trip to Tobruk and that was important. We would be going by army transport from point to point. The first stop was very rough. We "slept" in bivouacs, usually full of fleas. We were told at break-fast that camels were often kept in certain areas and shed their "flocks" in the process. We were also advised about scorpions having a preference for sleeping in boots or anywhere quiet. Desert rats were talked about, but I found them to be very pretty. The journey was tedious and very uncomfortable but, adversely, I did begin to quite like the desert and at the time things were quiet and German-less!

The same at Tobruk itself. Placed in high ground, overlooking a useful port and bay with beaches in plenty. The Signals were stationed immediately outside the town which had few inhabit-ants, barring troops and arms. There was a canteen in the town. I was checked in with George and given our instructions by a very polite Sergeant Major. As the town had been notably involved and changed hands several times, it had a worldy feeling of its own. We could and did go bathing there twice. I learnt to swim, in lovely warm waters, for the first time, taught by a Cecil Fischel who became my companion when we were captured later.

In the three weeks I was there until 20th June 1942, I noticed Cecil was ridiculed mercilessly and I felt angry with some of them for their ignorance. He was Jewish and more intelligent than they were, by far. His Dad came to England penniless and had to beg in the streets to start with. After a few years, he had a chain of stores.

We were given ammunition for our 303 rifles with no specific instructions and I really felt "in the war" and ready to go! Our duties were simple. "Be on call at all times." Tobruk had a mixed history since 1939 and in the course of which it had taken quite a walloping, being a strategically placed port in Libya and needed for supplies particularly.

I had my wireless operator's van and took a good look round. I did not see many civilians. I went to the NAAFI canteen which was well stocked, and bought some cigarettes – Italian ones. The food from our cooks was plain and wholesome – mostly corned beef turned into various offerings plus the cook's version of a pudding, if lucky. But after all, we were in a very hot spot in view of the continual bombing!

Various aircraft went over us and I took a pot shot at one or two, knowing they might be notorious "Stukas" which were venomous bombers as I understood from others in our unit. I was severely reprimanded. "They'll come back and bomb us!" "Woa! What are we here for?!" I didn't actually say that, only thought it.

Our unit was attached to the Royal Artillery responsible for anti aircraft. They had been very busy, but lately there had been a quiet period of about two weeks. Several of us, as I said, went bathing on the nearby shore but had to go through a chance of landmines there and back to our quarters for the privilege. It gave us the opportunity to get clean, too.

Chapter 9:

Capture!

It was not long before we heard rumours that the Germans were moving towards Tobruk in gradual stages, so when we heard shelling quite near we got ready for trouble. It came one morning, two days later, 20th June 1942 at breakfast when one of the shells split a rifle leaning against the wall near me. Suddenly there was panic. Our young officer on duty threw himself under a table, shaking like a lily, and a voice called out, "Does anyone here know how to use a Bren gun?" I panicked, then said, "Yes, I do." I had been on a weapon course soon after I won my stripe and had enjoyed it. Anyway, they found me one and gave me some ammunition and a partner to load for me. But it was the wrong ammunition!

We went out and settled in a place of some cover – not much – and started to load up. I suddenly realised a tank was approaching with a German visible, looking out of the top and I knew we had to put our hands up! With the right "ammo", I would probably have used it only to be blown away. Such is death!

In the process of being moved away by the Germans, with all the shelling going on from our allies the South Africans, a German soldier had been moved out of his tank and was being helped by his crew. One of his comrades waved for more assistance and we did our best to help the poor fellow who had almost lost a leg. I had always felt dizzy at the thought of such things, but that did not occur this time and never has since! Then all of us prisoners – about twenty – were moved on hurriedly whilst shells were landing all around. They transpired to have been sent by our allied forces doing their best! This ushering continued for what seemed an age and necessitated diving down on to the sand causing, I discovered later, a sore patch on one knee. That turned out to be a considerable nuisance later.

Before moving into a pen (a temporary holding pen made of corrugated iron and wire) after a longish journey, I did manage to nip into an empty shelter and found a lovely pair of officer's desert boots which became my saviour many a long time later. Good luck or observance? Divine intervention, probably! The pen was only a temporary one but it contained a large number of South African troops, black and white. They were very friendly and sociable for such a situation and we had a laugh or two in baiting the Jerries, who got quite aggressive and rattled the wires with bayonets and guns.

After a week or so, we were all moved to a very large camp near Benghazi. This camp was holding 4,000 to 5,000 prisoners and was manned entirely by Italian troops. It was very well set out with bivouacs and certain amenities such as medical facilities, including treatment for lice, that we had not been given before. I once was told Mussolini was making a call by the gates whilst on a tour of his fighting forces out there!

Cecil Fischel and I were still together and the camp was surrounded by Italian sentries with stands overlooking the wire fences. The food consisted of a bread roll a day plus a portion of soup containing unspecified meat. We had to collect it from a big kitchen. I made up my mind that being there was going to help my escape plans, undivulged even to Cecil, who I guessed would not be readily agreeable to such a scheme. I had thought, ever since capture, that a getaway in some way, somewhere would be achieved. So to keep active and fit as well as observant was necessary. Also needed was knowledge of the language. I therefore talked to the Italians in simple terms as many times as I possibly could. Cecil was content with spending his own time walking round for exercise – it was a large camp.

There was a central area for cooking, meeting and bartering. Entertainment was available sometimes by the prisoners themselves, as there was a lot of talent musically and theatrically available. There was also a medical section with a British officer in charge.

There was a swapping centre for the friendly exchange of belongings and parcel contents. This was a boon as I learnt more Italian (using the Latin base) to guide me. At school Latin had been the one subject I had failed in matriculation, as I did not appreciate the use of it at the time. So this availability meant I could "swap" inside or outside the camp! The Italians began to ask for items and I made a very good connection with a certain Sargenti Gerardi! I got to know him and his guards too on a friendly and laughing basis – and sometimes one of them sang a song. Cecil and I soon became quite well off – he became cashier and general cook and bottle washer. He had been a wonderful companion and his philosophy was a shrewd, if cautious, one. He also gave out any news, gossip and advice for various situations such as descriptions of the Italian way of living and their views on the war.

One night I heard suspicious noises. It was 2.30 am and I found that someone was cutting through the canvas of our bivouac. I let out the biggest yell I could muster and chased after the would-be thief. My pursuit was ineffective, but warned us both that people were aware of our bartering achievements!

I had noticed that certain chaps had paired up and that it was a "dark hair and blond" matter usually. Appearances seemed to decide the relationships. They were mostly good types, and often entertaining in the little shows they put on. They were not very kind though in talking of, or dealing with, the coloured men. I treated everyone the same way – why not? Always have.

I asked Gerardi if he knew a method of changing English money over to liras and he said, "Yes", he thought so, via the Arabs and would ask. He knew there would be a cut for him. Gerardi, after a day or two, told me that he had a deal if I wished and gave me the details, which I accepted with relish.

I had lately been troubled by lice in the hair, which really is a ghastly feeling. So we were delighted to find we could be de-loused at the medical centre. My knee had been getting worse and I seemed to be also feeling in low spirits. So I told the Medical Officer. He examined me there and then and announced, "This man is ill and must go to hospital!" So I was taken, with my belongings, right away to Benghazi Hospital. It was a rather grim looking place, but proved to be comfortable inside. I had with me the lira from Gerardi. Cecil was left with a useful amount of the rest of our belongings to mind and I hoped he would manage to take due care of himself and it.

As for me, the Medical Officer had said I had jaundice, dysentery and an infected knee. I was put in a room with about twelve beds, mine next to a window. On my other side was a South African coloured man whom I recall smiling at me. During the night I heard things dropping on beds – not mine, that night – which transpired to be bugs. Ugh! In the morning I told Matron (Italian) and made a fuss about it. She smiled pleasantly but said nothing. Later that day the whole room was disinfected, thank goodness for my modest use of Italian fuss.

The food was simple, mostly rice and bread with soup. I didn't feel like eating much, but did my best. The knee now started to get me worried rather, so I called Matron again and showed her the swelling. She called out and a doctor came. He took me to his surgery and opened the place in the knee with a pair of scissors! It shook me up in no uncertain manner, but it started to get better quickly and so did I! Crude expedience paid off!

I soon got hungry again, and the South African next to me offered me his rice. I at first declined with thanks and he said, "But you helped me once and I would like to return the kind-ness." "How did I help you then?" He said "You gave me two cigarettes in the camp" and smiled again. "What's your name then?" "Landra." "Mine's Gordon."

I got better so quickly that I was sent back to the camp, but to a different part. I was told we were being moved again. The next day I was walking round the wire to see if I knew any of the guards. I did in one instance and he threw over some cigarettes. Two packets! It was lucky for me, for the next day we were moved into the hold of a ship!

It was obviously a large ship, and it did seem rather crowded, judging by our hold. There was little room to spare and we all must have hoped that the journey was to be a brief one. But to where? I recognised familiar faces from the Benghazi camp, one in particular a Londoner called Barney. I had had bartering deals with him and he had seemed someone with whom it was best to be cautious. Maybe he thought the same about me? Anyway he approached me in a friendly enough way. "Hope to see you at the other end, eh, Gordon?" "Wherever", I said.

Food was sent down to us to help ourselves to; a sort of skilly, or gruel, and bread rolls. It was a large hold and I noticed what seemed to be a fastened door quite near my sleeping place. It turned out that there were steps down to another hold containing a stock of parcels. I had got friendly with an Australian near me and he said, "Let's git dahn, eh? Mate." "Right ho," said I and we ventured down cautiously. Some of it was food – tins of meat. So we took some – the "Aussie" said he had a tin opener in his kit.

As the voyage continued we found out the course taken as best we could, by hearsay and comments from the crew. After a few days, we were all ushered off the ship onto a dock lined with armed troops. We thought we were due to be mown down! But no, there was an Italian officer and he told us off severely for bad conduct on the way and that we would be sorry if there was a recurrence. But we would be given more freedom to see some of the view from the ship than before, he added.

That port was in Greece. We travelled for a long time along a rocky coast, and then mostly sea only until being disembarqued eventually at Bari, in southern Italy once again. Upon arrival there, we were marched through the streets between crowds of people who expressed their feelings vehemently; some spitting went on! After that we left the town and entered a new camp about three miles away. This looked much more agreeable with rows of huts, a grassy area and other parts separated off for staff etc. We had an English Sergeant Major in charge of us and he told us of strictness existing, and about a committee he had to advise him! Wow!

I got the lower bed of the two near to the back door in my hut, which had forty inmates. Similar food to that served up on the ship was brought round for us here too, but we were about to get Red Cross parcels soon! "Kriegsgefangen Post" accounting for the nickname "Kriegies" to all and sundry. The new camp was called Tuturano and, along the route to it on foot, I had noticed some very pleasant country nearby. The guards, however, were further away than the previous Benghazi camp and not quite so accessible as before. But my Italian was better and we had some swapping to be done! The first parcels had arrived. Our "committee", especially the Sergeant Major, was not keen on our fraternising with the guards and had also made a special enclosure for the "blacks" to be put in. They started to have us searched in case we were dealing with the guards or the "blacks". So it was like having Gestapo supervision within ourselves.

As the weather turned colder, they gave out some warm clothes and caps which looked rather like old French uniforms. 1943 approached and in no time we were using the clothes. I had a go with one of these uniforms and got through a gate to the Italian quarters by a bluff speedy approach and sharp "graze" (thanks)! I found myself mingling with them and it was two to three hours before they cheerfully moved me back!

That episode and another one when I was found in the "blacks" section got me one week's "confined to barracks" in our own POW camp! Anyway they had started playing football by now and I was in some demand for these games. The Italians were keen spectators – those off duty anyway.

In February we were moved further north to a camp in Fermo (Ascoli Piceno) and this was a huge building with its own enclosed sports area. I was initially put with NCOs and able to see out to this area, but soon moved to a very large building with lots of two storey beds. I previously had had a couple of clashes with two of the chaps in there near me, but was greeted by both in a friendly way and asked to play for their section team. That suited me very much. So, I said "Yes, anytime." It being a large building, I was able to see a lot that occurred and I was shocked at some of the sexual behaviour going on, quite brazenly. And the language was pretty strong. It seemed to be confined to a group in one corner not too far away. The discipline in this camp was misused indeed. They did have a large number of NCOs and a good percentage of regular soldiers, whose every other word appeared to be essentially four letters! Nothing I could do about that, though. Hollywood, here we come!

Chapter 10:

Escape

I was able to keep myself active very easily. Somewhere in the camp there was a secret wireless and we heard that our lads had landed further south – in a big way. Spirits were high indeed. I had made some contact with the Italians via bartering and football. One of them joked about freedom for the English. So I asked him where I could go locally if that happened and he told me of a local family who hated the "Tedeski! (Germans). I listened very carefully and wrote down the details on a piece of cardboard. Meanwhile, I played quite a lot of football and once for the "Signals" - my RSM from Tobruk asked me! I was also asked by Jonah, a regular Royal Artillery Sergeant, as big as a bull, to play for England! Jonah also asked me if I would try to escape with him. I said, "Why?" He said I would help with the Italians. I said, "What?" thinking, "With the women?" He made a lewd remark and that decided me. "No thanks, Jonah." And that was that...... for the time being.

Another day or two later a Life Guardsman called Jim Blay – a quiet, tall man – asked me if he could join me if I tried to escape. I had observed him before and said "Yes, if you'll keep it quiet and let me be the boss, I'll consider it, Jim."

We were well informed in warlike ways and methods. I had a good think about what I'd said to Jim and reflected on some of the people I had met so far. Barney was one, and his ways obvious – he was part of a big bookmaker family in Elephant & Castle, the knees-up area of London and pretty lively with it too. He was bound to be wide – No, not him... the Aussie man – rather too variable, and a different outlook – no. Jonah – ouch! – no. Jim?

Coldstream Guardsman whose regiments had fought very hard at Tobruk, quiet, strong and tall, and a Londoner who had gone to the same school as Vera Lynn. I talked to him often now and would have to make a decision quickly when it came. I thought about that noisy and sordid group in my vicinity, on their ways and habits.

I had occasion to refer to my memories of childhood when I was eight years old, and recalled another awful time when two older boys of about thirteen and sixteen had collared me in a quiet part of Beddington Park, with thickish woods nearby, and pulled off my shorts. One held my arms behind me and the other younger one sat on my legs and tickled my penis until I thought I was going mad (being extremely ticklish). "We'll stop if you are very nice to us," said the older and taller boy. So I had to masturbate them both twice before being freed – awful! One of them even came round to my house some time later, to try to get me to come out again with them, blackmailing me with threats of what he would tell my parents. I refused. Not long after that, I was relieved to hear that that boy's family had moved out of the country.

The group in the POW camp had seemed to have something very suspiciously like that going on several times. My turn in the park had seemed to go on forever and I shall never forget it, or their gang. In any case we planned to escape in a few days' time.

Two or three days after speaking to Jim again, we were told that we were going to be allowed certain freedoms on restrictions which meant that we might get the chance to go outside the camp. There was a great deal of talk about how well our forces were faring in the invasion and were moving gradually more to the north, pushing the Germans back. The general attitude of the Italians was improving towards us. We were allowed out in groups of twenty or so with armed guards for an hour or two.

On the first trip out Jim and I took as good a look around as we could without making too much of a show of it. The country was lovely, with plenty of cover, trees and shrubs in abundance and there was the village of Fermo not far away, higher up as villages were in such areas. The next time we had brought with us as many items as we could comfortably manage and then lingered around near a place that we had selected as suitable for our plans. When our guards' attention was divided, we rustled up some shrubbery to give us extra cover and made a good hideout under some trees. We then kept absolutely quiet and still, until all the rest of the party had gone. The guards had taken a cursory look around but seemed more interested in chatting than us. Bingo! We stayed put until dusk and the church bells sounded from Fermo.

We made our way slowly in the direction previously advised by our friend the sentry and found some sleep; it was really lovely in the morning and we could hear a woman singing in a far-off field, happy with her work, melodious and peaceful. No one would think there was a war involved with our three countries, or that we were anything but local labourers going to Fermo.

We were in a hedged lane which led to another hard lane leading to the village and turned right going away from it. After a while we came across a young boy aged about eight, I guessed. (After this, you must permit me to write everything in English with occasional plunges into Italian when I feel more certain of the spelling!)

He stared at us and when we had just passed him, he said, "Bon giorno," to which I replied likewise. He smiled broadly and asked where we were going. I told him Fermo and he said, "Inglese?" I said, "Yes." "What are you doing here?" he asked. I told him we were escaped prisoners and didn't know where to go, could he help? His eyes lit up and he told us we could go to his house and perhaps his mother could help. So we followed him, all the time carefully keeping watch for other persons.

When we came to his house, about a mile further on, he called, "Mamma" and a pretty woman of about thirty came to the door. "Si?" He rattled on in quick reply and great length. "Non!" "Non?" "Non. Non!" Oscali and his mother explained in much detail – then smiled at us in an apologetic way.

Oscali told us his mother was terrified that the Germans, who were by the sea, would punish us all if they allowed us to stay. He added that he had an uncle who might be of use, as he hated the Tedeski. He pulled an angry face to illustrate! This boy was obviously very bright, and wanted to be a help. "Se ciama Luigi" He's called Luigi. I told him I was called Gordon and my friend, Jim. "Andiamo" (Let's go!).

So we followed him, over hilly country, winding here and there for two or three miles until we came to a little group of mixed buildings, concealed by trees, but opening out on to a glorious view at the rear. A rather fierce man with a reddish countenance glowered at us. Oscali explained the story so far and the old man's eyes brightened and he laughed, "Si praego". And he proceeded to show us their small farm and a barn where we could sleep, all with great gusto and a windmill of waving arms! Oscali (Cisbani was his surname) said, "Arrivadechi" and that he would come again soon. I thought that we would be very comfortable in these quarters.

Whilst we were staying at Luigi's, Oscali had said that we could help some friends nearby who had work to do including making wine. This appealed to me very much. The next few days were very interesting and passed quickly. One day we spent helping with the wine, stamping on the grapes with the others who were local friends and relatives. Afterwards we had supper with chicken and tomato with pasta. We drank the wine just made and it was very sweet.

Another day we ventured into Fermo – Jim did not really approve – and had a drink in a wine parlour which had several German soldiers in it, being festive. Jim said nothing but I kept up a simple stream of Italian words, sounds and gestures when I thought it was warranted!

Also during this visit we went to another little farm and the owner was modestly English-speaking. He wanted to know if we could do business when I got home? Very positive and complimentary!

Another time we had a risky escape! Luigi had arranged for us to stay overnight at the house of one of his aunts. When the small hours came and we were quietly sleeping, there was a tap on the shoulder from the lady of the house and she whispered, "Fascisti"! We immediately were alerted, and waited to see the next move. She pointed to the window and made a gesture to us to "get out" urgently. Loud kicks and shouting followed, so we climbed out of the window and on to the sloping roof to hear excited babble down below. We slid down away from the furore and pelted away as fast as we could into the fields. My officer's boots came in usefully – they were rubber-soled. Pandemonium followed us but we'd had plenty of space and time in the end. The Fascisti never saw us, so all was okay for our hosts! It was the final episode of that period with Luigi and it turned out fortunately for us.

One auspicious day we were told to take cover down in the woods. Soon after, a little boy came down crying excitedly, "Inglese!" I said, "No! Tedeski?" He said, "No – Inglese!! Andiamo!" So we went back up and saw three soldiers talking to Luigi and others gathered around. One said, "I'm Captain Allen and we're looking for people like you!!"

He was about my age and his two companions were younger. They all had an efficient air about them and their greetings were assuring. Captain Allen explained that they were part of a very special force of paratroopers who had personal instructions to collect up the many POWs who had taken advantage of the lull in enmity the Italians had shown since our successful landing in their country by allied troops. Marvellous!

He further enthused to such an extent, "Churchill has shown such keenness since our success in landing on these shores that his well-known determination and sleeplessness will not rest until we have made our maximum effort."

He gave an explicit guide to the plan involved which entailed following a nearby river down to the estuary, or near it, where the Germans had a base on the coastal road going north and south. He did not stay long, and the three went off quickly, Allen saying that we would no doubt meet him soon!

Jim and I were so delighted but regretted leaving our Italian friends so hastily, but this was war. After all the help that was given to us, friendliness and security, it was hard indeed.

Whilst on the run, our thoughts had often turned to those POWs whom we had left behind. By now some of them would know that we had escaped. How did they feel about that? Would I ever see any of them again? Sadly, I never did. They melted away, once the war was over. Indeed a great many were killed in an aircraft accident on their way to Germany. A whole planeload of men met their deaths. It was a truly shocking event. It was all the more poignant for me as I had great concerns over the whereabouts of my friend, Cecil Fischel, and I hope that he did not perish along with them.

Chapter 11:

Italy August 1943 – Goodbye Luigi

"The time has come for us to leave – very soon, Jim".

"Now?"

"Yes. Let's see what we have to take … I say …"

"What are we going to tell Luigi?"

"Nothing. Don't be so talkative."

"Do you think that's best?"

"Sure thing."

"You mean just walk out?"

"Why not? If we tell him anything he'll as likely as not hand us over to the Fascists now we are leaving. Here he is now. Make it look casual – as if we are out for a stroll. If he asks where we're going I'll say Manzano to buy some cigarettes."

And so we left …. We made for the open country. The towns and villages were too full of Fascists, and the Germans might pass at any time. There had been reports that some were staying in Manzano – it might have been just another rumour but we weren't taking any chances. We stopped and Jim rolled a cigarette. I felt that we hadn't been quite fair to poor old Luigi – we had stayed with him for three weeks and he was a very good fellow when he was drunk!

One night he had brought us back some cigarettes – the price was high, but we had money then.

"See! Luigi is good to you. Popolari at five lire a packet! I can get ten lire in Rome, but Luigi is good."

We didn't tell him to go to Rome and take his Popolari with him!

Then there was the night we had made the wine, and Luigi had fried a chicken – we talked and drank until morning. He was a grand fellow all right. The next morning he threw a chair at his mother. He was sober again.

The river transpired to be a large varying spring, sometimes quite deep but with fair-sized shallow parts and plenty of woodland on either side. We had reckoned on it being five to six miles to the sea. We called at a farm first off to the left and were given food willingly enough, but no offer of somewhere to sleep so we said "thanks" and went on. Captain Allen had told me that there should be many involved, he hoped. He had given out that, as it was a personal directive from Winston Churchill, all help would be given to this plan – to pick us all up on the next Saturday - which was three days ahead!

Later that day I said to Jim that I had heard something ahead and I left him to keep watch as I went on ahead to investigate. As I approached it seemed to be a group of people, so I crept forward for some fifty yards, very slowly indeed. Then I took the plunge and went right up to them saying, "Bon giorno" in my best Italian voice. They all turned quickly, guns ready. "Ah! Huntington," Captain Allen said, "Well done! I want you to stay in a spot further up to prevent any more people going further towards the sea. I agreed readily and went back to Jim and told him to wait near me at the spot required.

Nothing much happened for a while, then several different people came and did as they were told except one who asked me on what authority I acted, and in a rude tone said he was an officer and that he would report me to the Captain later and see that I was charged. I insisted and he went away a very angry man!

Later that day a South African officer came – at least I thought that was what he was –and I told him, after seeing how useful he could be to us, that I'd like him to stay nearby with Jim. Next day would be only one day before the crucial one. He agreed readily, he having told me of his bushcraft skills through living in a hunting area in South Africa. So now we were three! He was called Pat.

The next day was spent similarly with Jim and the South African officer providing food they had elicited locally from some generous Italians, one being a woman called an unusual name "Pasquelina", which made us giggle. We thought it a beautiful name with a lovely ring to it when said with their musical pronunciation. She was a large, jolly lady and very friendly.

By the time Saturday evening had come we were primed up for dusk and for things to happen. It had transpired that Pat was better-informed and said we could move forward a little, being quite near to the coast already. Accordingly, we did find a very suitable cover – a ridge with thickish hedge parts. Whilst we were there we could continually hear noises inland and the barking of dogs made me wonder if it might be heard by the Germans! But it went on increasingly and with dusk upon us, suddenly chaos occurred and voices in German, then shots quite close. None of us moved, but stayed still behind the bushy hedge. We had to keep absolutely still for an age and we heard German voices just the other side of the hedge! Pausing, arguing then fading inland. Phew!

We stayed put until the babble and barking ceased and then discussed what to do in a nearby woodland area (Pat's bushcraft coming in useful again) in quiet voices. It was decided to move on that day and get as far as we could manage. Darkness was falling and we needed to find somewhere to sleep. We moved up the hill, parallel with the sea.

We could now only converse in whispers! "What next?" I asked. "I think find somewhere to sleep", said Pat. "That won't be easy at this time of the evening" I said. Then he told me that if we tried again next night, we could be picked up then, perhaps. Jim and I were both willing to have a try – we presumed that Pat had had prior information and left it at that. We moved cautiously uphill for about a mile, then found a largish group of dwellings. We had struck lucky! The occupants quietly accepted us, and obviously were keen to help us. They must have heard all the noise and shots.

Two to three hundred POWs had been expected to join us on this careful scheme to take us home. The Prime Minister knew that we needed more experienced men back at home to build the Army for greater things. I believed that God had helped us to be still then behind the cover of the hedges and prayed we could benefit from his benevolence! If we tried again tomorrow, and we only had a short time now, we should have to be in a safer place than this. The prayer must have helped as we found ourselves quite early that evening in the home of the Illuminati family.

The farmer opened the door and appeared friendly. We could sleep in his barn.

"We have no blankets, but we will find coats for you. Who are you?"

"English. Prisoners. We have escaped from the Germans."

"The Germans are bad. We are made poor by them. Come inside and eat with us."

I thanked him and we all sat down in silence.

"Will you have wine?" his wife smiled kindly, "And some food?"

We all smiled.

"Give it to them, Milena."

"Madonna mia! We are not so poor that they cannot share our wine and food."

"Fine boys! Where are you going? We have these two daughters", Mama indicated with a proud gesture.

"To Termoli, Signora", not wishing to betray our plans.

"By foot?"

"Yes."

"It is a long way."

"Yes. We travel day by day." Sometimes we stop at a contradini and work. If we can we will leave very early tomorrow and continue our journey. We find it best to travel when it is cooler."

Where will you find food tomorrow?"

"The contradinis are always good to us."

"Fine boys! I have a son. He may be dead. Who knows? It is a cruel life."

Someone sitting by the fire sighed. It was a girl. She was beautiful. I smiled at her.

"What is your name?"

"Santina."

"A beautiful name."

She sighed again. We finished our cigarettes and prepared to leave for bed.

"Oh, no." cried Milena. "It is early. Please stay."

"But you must be tired. You work so hard."

"If we didn't work we would die. It is nothing. All my life I have worked."

She held something in her hand.

"What is that?"

"A shoe. It is Santina's. She believes it is lucky," said her mother.

"How do you know?"

"Because it is Santina's!"

They laughed happily and gathered around us. To the lace of the shoe was attached a key. Santina and Milena held the key with their forefingers – one on each end. The shoe was suspended.

"Black for luck" said Santina. "If the black shoe turns, you will have luck on your journey. If it stays still, you will not."

They tried it twice. Twice the black shoe turned.

"Indeed we shall soon be home, then!" I cried.

"God pray you will. I give you my blessing."

"Thank you. We will remember. We must sleep now. We are very grateful for your kindness."

"It is nothing. Good night and good luck."

"Buon voyagio" said Santina.

"Good night."

"Good night."

We made ourselves comfortable in the barn. The night was warm.

"Well? Only a few hours to go and then – who knows?"

"Who knows? Shall I roll another fag?"

"Okay."

"What was it she said?"

"Who?"

"Santina."

"About what?"

"The shoe!"

"Oh, nothing much," I said. "These people are simple – and superstitious. She said if the shoe turned we would have luck."

"The black shoe did turn, too. Perhaps we will have luck."

"I hope so, don't you? Good night."

"Good night."

"Good night. What time is it?"

"Nine o'clock. We've got four hours."

There was no fear of oversleeping. It was impossible to sleep. At one o'clock Jim shook me.

"It's time."

"Yes. I haven't slept, has either of you?"

"No."

"No."

After walking cautiously for a couple of miles, we made our way quietly to the beach. We crossed the road and the sea roared ahead of us. We hid in the bushes by the shore and watched the sea. It made strange sounds – a black mysterious monster – uncontrollable and terrible, it seemed.

Another hour went by.

"Can you hear anything, either of you?"

"No. Can you?"

"I thought I heard vehicles", said Pat who had also mentioned looking out for a shining light.

"It's the sea."

"Yes, it's the sea, I suppose."

"What's the time?"

"Two o'clock. Keep waiting."

"Wish we had a smoke."

It seemed like an age, and then Jim grabbed my shoulder fiercely.

"There's something there," he whispered hoarsely.

"I can't see anything."

"I can! I can!"

"My eyes aren't right. What is it?" said Pat.

"I think it's a boat!"

"My God, are you sure?"

"Yes it's a boat! A boat! A boat!"

Pat rushed to the water's edge excitedly.

"Keep back, Jim – just in case."

"Are you English?" a voice came from the blackness, seeming miles away.

"You got the message then? Good chap, you'll soon be home."

A motor torpedo boat (MTB) loomed up quite soon. Willing hands helped us aboard – the engine awoke with a steady roar.

And so we left – three saved chaps on the right side again!

As soon as we were aboard I could see it was not an MTB but something larger and more pugnacious - a frigate, I think. We were looked after very well – beds, food and clothes as far as they were able to help. It was a happy journey for us, although peppered by air attacks and, later, threats from rumoured submarines in the neighbourhood.

Pat was landed at an earlier stop and Jim and I were taken to Bari for the second time. There we were questioned very thoroughly and kitted out with fresh clothing – I was pleased to see that my uniform was Canadian colour khaki! – and to be paid in the old rate of liras to the pound on any money we had. This latter item helped me more than Jim, who had not bartered ever.

In Bari we could walk about where we cared to, and this time met lots of children, who were asking for anything at all; obviously being so poor under German supervision. Poor kids, I thought! We were soon told that a ship would be taking us over and back again to North Africa prior to going back to England ASAP. I glowed at the prospect....

We went "tout de suite" across the Mediterranean to Tunis and thence on to a goods train for a very lengthy journey to Algiers with few comforts on the way, except that we were going home.

It was interesting to see the locality, and the mountain views at night were very dramatic. Throughout the journey, some hundreds of miles, we were pestered at frequent stops by Arabs some of whom looked cadaverous, or even murderous at times, and asked for "back-sheesh" which means money, or anything in fact – just give. On reflection, a very surreal trip, but free of charge.

On arrival in Algiers, a tumultuous city, we were transported to a British military base near the coast on the outskirts. In getting there, I met a chap called Ray who seemed very lively and came from the Isle of Man. He and I were billeted in the same block on arrival.

Jim was preoccupied with two guardsmen he had met, too, so on Ray's invitation, we explored together. He had a smattering of French, as had I, and we met a couple of Free French lady privates after he had asked them where the nearest cinema was nearby. They joined us to see a Laurel & Hardy film showing there in an absolutely crowded cinema. We noticed that the fat one, Hardy, got the "boos", perhaps because he slapped and bullied Laurel so much. Anyway, a riot started down near the front and fighting began amidst absolute bedlam, so we scooted out! We found a suitable wine house instead and tested our French. The French ladies were both very friendly and extremely good company.

Then, whilst wandering near the base down by the coast, I found some empty holiday houses and one of them was not locked! So back at the base I told Ray and Jim and we decided to try sleeping there until we were leaving for our ship home. It was a very nice sort of holiday to have, as we did... we had nothing to do except go for meals until then.

Boarding ship, a large one, we were given quarters below deck with bunks suspended from the ceiling and it was very crowded with men like me going home. There was no work to do, so we had time on our hands. There were constant rumours about submarines again, as this was a dangerous route and circumstance. I suggested to Jim that we could sleep in a lifeboat and get some fresh air as well, and so for the most part we did! The journey was only a few days and then there was Liverpool!

Chapter 12:

War in Words

My father, Harold Huntington, was a careful, astute man. Tidy and methodical in nature, he applied his business-like approach to everything in life. Thus I was delighted to discover that, whilst I was in the Army, he meticulously filed much of the correspondence pertaining to the war. In particular, I was thrilled to find that he had kept the letters I had sent home. These letters were sent to my beloved family and usually took months to reach their destination. Indeed, when I wrote them, I did not know whether my family were safe and well or whether they had been badly affected by the war.

There follows a chronological history of written documentation from parties including the Army, The British Red Cross Society, the Vatican War Enquiry Department, and from me, as a prisoner of war.

Army Form E. 622

Agreement to be made by an officer or man of the Territorial Army on undertaking the obligation under Section 13 (2) (b) of the Territorial and Reserve Forces Act, 1907.

I (No.) 2575957.   *(Rank) Sgmn.*

(Name) Huntington. G. H.

of the (Unit) The London Divisional Signals. (City of London Signals) T.A.

do hereby agree to come up for service for purposes of defence at any place in the United Kingdom where my services may be required, under Section 13 (2) (b) of the Territorial and Reserve Forces Act, 1907, subject to the conditions printed on the back hereof.

....
(Signature of Officer or Man.)

....
(Signature of Witness.)

....
(Signature of Commanding Officer.)

20, ATKINS RD., CLAPHAM PARK, S.W. 12.
(Station)

Date ....

(SEE BACK.)

CONDITIONS OF SPECIAL AGREEMENT UNDERTAKEN BY AN OFFICER OR MAN OF THE TERRITORIAL ARMY, UNDER SECTION 13 (2) (b) OF THE TERRITORIAL AND RESERVE FORCES ACT, 1907.

(A.) Every officer or man who undertakes the obligation under Section 13(2) (b) of the Territorial and Reserve Forces Act, 1907, will be required to sign an Agreement on Army Form E. 622, in the presence of an officer of the Unit.

(B.) He will engage to come up for actual military service for purposes of defence when called upon to do so under the authority of the Secretary of State in the United Kingdom, even though no order calling out the Territorial Army for actual military service is in force at the time.

(C.) When called out on such service he will retain the rank which he held in the Territorial Army.

(D.) This agreement will remain in force so long as he is serving in the Territorial Army.

(E.) He will, if called out and employed under this agreement for service in case of emergency, receive as soon as possible after reporting himself for duty, provided that he is then fit for service, the gratuity of £5 which is given to men of the Territorial Army on embodiment. (Note.- If the Territorial Army is embodied while he is so serving he will not be eligible for a second £5 gratuity.)

(F.) When on such service he will receive the pay and allowances issuable to a regular officer or soldier of the corresponding rank and arm, including, in the case of warrant officers, non-commissioned officers and men, family allowance (if eligible).

(G.) In the event of his being killed, wounded or disabled while on such service, he or his dependents will be eligible for pension or gratuity under the same conditions as if the Territorial Army were embodied.

Army Form E. 518

RESERVE AND AUXILIARY FORCES ACT, 1939.
TERRITORIAL ARMY.

CALLING OUT NOTICE.

To: -

Name *G. H. Huntington*

Rank .... Army Number: 2575957

Regt. or Corps: The London Divisional Signals (City of London Signals) T.A.

In pursuance of directions given by the Secretary of State for War in accordance with an Order in Council made under Section 1 of the above-mentioned Act, you are hereby notified that you are called out for military service commencing from ....19..., and for this purpose you are required to join The London Divisional Signals, (City of London Signals), at... AT ONCE on that day.

Should you not present yourself on that day you will be liable to be proceeded against.

Stamp of Officer Commanding Unit.
Major Adjutant
The London Divisional Signals,
(City of London Signals) T.A.

Place: 20, Atkins Road, Clapham Park, SW 12.
Date: 1 Sept 1939

Letter I wrote to my father, in pencil.

Sigmn Huntington
2575957
2 Coy 1 Holding Bn.
Catterick Camp
Yorks

8th Feb 1942

Dear Dad,

Many thanks for the razor which was a surprise for me. As a matter of fact, I have been spending all the morning trying to change mine at the QM as three-holed blades are the only blades available at the NAAFI. So it was with great pleasure that I found a razor in your parcel which arrived intact.

I have written previously of my feelings upon leaving you last week and I hope you understand that I will miss you all very much. I hope you are spared as many discomforts as possible till the end of the war. Certainly it looks as though there will be no No.2 Battle of Britain for a while. In any event – good luck. I have not departed yet and perhaps will not do so for a while – even there is the possibility, as yet faint, of another leave. In which case there is the happiness of seeing you all again mixed with the parting once again. Still – that is the war.

I remembered to send Mother a telegram yesterday wishing her many happy returns and I reiterate the message. She is young yet.

Usually in my letters comes a request – at least quite often. This time I am not pleading that I have no money. I have. But should I go away I want something to fall back on.

I have two pounds now and I want you to send me a pound or two for a reserve and take it from my 7/- a week allotment. My a/c is clear up to 2 Feb of this year, Dad – and I don't want to get stranded in Cairo or somewhere like that and not have a note or two! Did the Pru. pay my rise this month or not?

I want Mother to put all the money from them into the P. Office – I shall be able to save a good deal abroad as they pay us more I think. At least, that is the general opinion. In any case I would be 3 or 4 months on a boat and they only pay us 10/- a week then. So the rest would go to my credit, which is no good to me if I am in need of some money suddenly.

Well Dad – I wish you once again all the best, and please give all my love to Mother and the boys.

Your son
Gordon

POST OFFICE TELEGRAM

25th April '42

Will cable £10 Barclays
Cairo
Huntington

Air Mail Letter to Mr and Mrs H Huntington, 32 Crichton Avenue, Wallington, Surrey, England. This letter contains the secret code, telling my parents that I am in Tobruk.

From Sigmn Huntington
2575957
4 A.A. Signals
M.E.F.

1/5/42
Received 9 July 1942

Dear Mother & Dad,

This is a quick letter to let you know my new address, to which I have arrived after a unique journey over many miles! The more I see the more I am convinced that we will win out here, so, let's see a little action back home!

I expect my cable came as a surprise to you the other day – I required the money to open a bank a/c for all the money I will save during the next few months. Don't worry – I cannot possibly spend £10 out here. Best ways of reaching me are EMF telegram, Airgraph and Air Mail. If you should be able to buy a small primus stove (portable) that will take up very little room then that is the best thing I could possibly have in this country – and then I will be able to make tea now and again when I feel like it!

How are the boys? Tell Douglas I am not able to send him a birthday present but wish him many happy returns. How is Ken getting on at the factory? And I hope you both are quite well and cheerful.

Jane told me of her liberal increment. I trust she will keep on the straight and narrow! Give her my love too...

What does Edna's ring look like? I have been wondering that for weeks. Tell her from me that I am thinking of her all the time. I will be writing regularly to her as well as to you.

My love to you all.

Gordon

PS. I am quite fit.

Air Mail Letter to my brother, K. Huntington Esq., 32 Crichton Avenue, Wallington, Surrey, England.

From Sigmn Huntington 2575957
68th Heavy A.A.RGT Signal
M.E.F.

4 May 42
Received date unknown

Dear Douglas and Ken,

It is not often that I write to you two brats but here goes... I have travelled many thousands of miles now and seen many strange things. In fact I am a man of experience so when I return I expect you to pay me a little respect – and rest upon my words of wisdom.

How are you both? I expect Douglas is still designing the new world on little pieces of paper - and Kenny making packets of money in business. Anyway I hope you are both quite OK – I myself am not so bad thank you very much. Don't forget to shut the door as you go out. I had a very pleasant fortnight in Durban and was treated very kindly by the people there. Derek and Ian were quite near to me but I was not allowed to go and see them. Some friends I made there offered to take me to see them but it was not possible to get a pass.

I hope you are both quite happy and well – please give my love to Mother and Dad. Tell them to write to the above address until they hear again from me.

Much love,

Gordon

P.S. If you can send a primus stove it would be extremely useful.

G.

MILITARY AIRGRAPH SERVICE AUTHORISED BY EGYPTIAN POSTAL ADMINISTRATION

To H. Huntington Esq.

Sender's Address:
2575957 SGM Huntington G.H.
Signal Section
68 Heavy A.A. Regt.
M.E.F.

9 May 1942

Dear Dad,

I wonder how many letters you have had from me so far? I have had none yet but I really don't expect any for a while. The best way of getting in touch with me is by this service or Air Mail – so if you want to get a speedy answer try the old "Par Avion"!

Just now I am doing more or less the same work as I was at home but under slightly different conditions. The fellows in this section are a better crowd than those I was with before and have made the "settling down" part much easier. Whilst on the ship I got friendly with four other fellows and we determined to stick together for a posting – but we missed our chance and I was posted with George Wheeler to this regiment. As he was one of the four I suppose there isn't much to grumble at.

I am very anxious to hear from you at home, telling me all the news, how everyone is, and what you think of this and that! Believe me, I shall jump into the air for joy when a letter does come. Did you get a surprise when my special Marconi arrived? I hope you had no difficulty about cabling the money. I shall apply to increase my allotment to 2/6d per day starting from September, so warn Mother that she might hear from the Paymaster in August. Give my love to

Mother and, look after her well – also Ken and Douglas. Once again many happy returns to Douglas, and I'd better say to you as well Dad! Tell Edna I am writing.

Yours affectionately

P.S. I can do with a primus stove!

Gordon

MILITARY AIRGRAPH SERVICE AUTHORISED BY EGYPTIAN POSTAL ADMINISTRATION

To Mrs H. Huntington

Sender's Address:
2575957 SIGM Huntington G.H.
Signals
68th Heavy A.A. Regt.
M.E.F.

17 May 1942

My dear Mother,

I believe it is time I wrote to you to tell you that I am quite all right – but waiting to hear from you. You should have received a telegram stating my address the other day – either you or Edna anyway. I hope you will all make use of this Airgraph Service as it is very quick - I shall try to write one home every few days. Please don't send me any money at all unless I should specifically ask for some, which is unlikely. Doesn't that sound strange coming from me? I am a new man! Life is altogether different out here – it is hot and dry. But it is easy to get acclimatised, and I now feel as if I have been here for years. Yesterday I wrote to Hilda and I am going to write to Grandma, also to the Huntingtons as soon as I can. Please give my love to Dad and the boys, and tell Douglas that I have some stamps that I will send to him- so he had better start collecting right now. Kenny had better wear any clothes of mine that fit him, except my brown shoes, and the sports jacket. Also the socks! I don't want to walk about in my birthday suit when I get back, so perhaps he had better go easy on the trousers too! Tell him not to sit down too much, and if he is asked why he doesn't want to, then he had better say why. Fool! All my love to you all dear.

Your affectionate son

Gordon

MILITARY AIRGRAPH SERVICE AUTHORISED BY EGYPTIAN POSTAL ADMINISTRATION

To Mrs H. Huntington

Sender's Address:
2575957 SIGM Huntington G.H.
Signals 68th Heavy A.A. Regt.
M.E.F.

24th May 1942

Mother dear,

If you should be writing to me on one of these airgraphs I suggest that you should print it out! Otherwise I shall not be able to read it.

I am still quite OK and happy enough where I am. My main worry is the mosquitoes at night time; the flies during the day.

It has occurred to me that I could do with a set of chessmen and board if you can possibly send one out to me dear. I play quite a lot of chess here against George and one or two others. I shall be able to flummox Dad after the war with many a clever move!

I shall be very glad to hear from you all – I am sending Douglas foreign stamps via Edna and will you ask him to save them if he doesn't want them himself? Give my love to Dad and the boys dear and look after yourself. I received confirmation of the £10 from Barclays Bank. Thank you for promptness in sending it.

Lots of love

Gordon

Air Mail Letter to H. Huntington Esq., 23 Crichton Avenue, Wallington, Surrey, England.

From Sigmn Huntington 2575957
68th Hvy A.A. (Signal Section) Regt
M.E.F.

24th May 42
Received date unknown

Dear Dad,

I think it is your turn to be blessed with a letter from Wandering Willy! How are you? And how is business? Many thanks for replying so promptly to my cable. I am sorry that it had to be rather to the point but, being a special cable, it was rather expensive to elaborate. Anyway it gave you an indication as to my whereabouts at the time. My reason for asking for the money was to have it in the bank, or in a cheque form as a standby for emergency, pay days being irregular etc.

Many thanks also for your letter regarding my engagement to Edna – I have no doubt you realise how pleased I was to receive your good wishes. We had been discussing it throughout my leave and decided practically at the last minute that we wanted to be engaged. My only regret is that I do not know what the ring looks like and was not able to do the thing quite as convention demands. However I am happy – I just hope everyone else is too!

I want you to encourage Douglas as much as possible in draughts-manship Dad – I was thinking the other day that he seems to have an inclination towards that – judging by his drawing and interest in plans. It will do him no harm to be encouraged anyway – he is at the age where the seed can be best sewn. Pardon my sonly advice old boy!

And keep Ken where he is if you possibly can – if he can study engi-neering I have something to talk to him about after the war!

Give my love to Mother and the other two fellows – wishing you a happy birthday and many to follow.

Gordon

I find after all that I am able to continue, but I apologise for the rough and ready stationery!

I want you to remember me to Grandma and Hilda. Also Vandy. Tell them that I often think of them – and that the war will be over soon.

I have fairly rapidly got used to a different climate and I like the open air life very much.

Well darlings I must stop now – soon you will get a proper letter and not one in pieces as this!

Fondest love,

Gordon
P.S. Best post Airgraphs or Airmail.

MILITARY AIRGRAPH SERVICE AUTHORISED BY EGYPTIAN POSTAL ADMINISTRATION

To Mrs H. Huntington

Sender's Address:
SIGM Huntington G.H.
Signals 68th Heavy A.A. Regt.
M.E.F.

25th May 1942

My dear Mother,

I am writing these letters now, fast upon each other, in case I should not be able to write so many later on. Indeed I am being a good boy because this week I have written to Grandma, Grandpa, Hilda and Eddy's wife on top of my usual letters to you and Edna. You remember French don't you? The chap who phoned up several times and delighted you by his thinking you sounded like my sister! I wrote to him as well.

Ask Dad this question…. Punctuate "Mary went into the wood undressed". Of course the answer is there should be a dash after Mary but don't tell him straight away. Coo! I done it now.

Well dear I am quite well and I send you lots of love.

Gordon

MILITARY AIRGRAPH SERVICE AUTHORISED BY EGYPTIAN POSTAL ADMINISTRATION

To H. Huntington Esq.

Sender's Address:
SGM Huntington 2575957
Signals 68th Heavy A.A. Regt.
M.E.F.

6th June 1942

Dear Dad,

I was delighted to receive three letters from home today. Keep it up! I am greedy for news. Of especial interest was the fact that a battle royal has finally been waged with the Reluctant Dragon – you will win and you will never regret the fight. I am sure of that. I am also proud – I don't like dragons. Even less do I like flies. They are my enemies! By your next letter I should know the outcome of it all – please let me know as soon as possible.

I am writing to Mother tonight, so she will not mind much if I send my love and is no more in this letter. I am quite OK. Received 17 letters today. One enclosed £2 which I once wanted but is now pleasant to look at. The £10 cabled is in the process of reaching me but I will not draw the cheque after all. It is merely for emergency. I was glad to receive Auntie Doris' address and she will receive a letter soon.

Well Dad – all the best! My love to Mother and the boys.

Your affectionate son.

Gordon

(P.S. A HAPPY 24th!!)

MILITARY AIRGRAPH SERVICE AUTHORISED BY EGYPTIAN POSTAL ADMINISTRATION

To Mrs H. Huntington

Sender's Address:
SGM Huntington 2575957
Signals 68th Heavy A.A. Regt.
M.E.F.

6th June 1942

My dear Mother,

Firstly I am quite all right and very happy. You must not worry at all dear – there is nothing to worry about. I don't want you to be in any doubt about one thing – very soon everything will be straightened out and you will say that you thought this and that – and all the time it was something else! And you had no need to worry at all! So – have no fear my dear. The corner has been turned – it is only a matter of time before I don my bowler hat and read the "Times" upside down – third class. I have written to Dad and told him how pleased I was to learn that he has taken the plunge. You must be pleased too.

I would like you to let me have a statement of accounts up to 31st May – just for my own little book. Can you oblige?

I send my love to you – take care of yourself and once again – don't worry!

Dad's letter should arrive simultaneously – should it not I wish him a happy birthday.

Your loving son,

Gordon

MILITARY AIRGRAPH SERVICE AUTHORISED BY EGYPTIAN POSTAL ADMINISTRATION

To Mr and Mrs H. Huntington

Sender's Address:
SGM Huntington 2575957
Signals 68th Heavy A.A. Regt.
M.E.F.

9ᵗʰ June 1942

Dear Mother and Dad,

I received your airgraph today dated 7th May. You now have my full address so I expect to get no trouble with mail in future. I have been fortunate to date as regards almost everything. My post arrived three days ago with three letters from you, the last one dated 5th March. My everyday life suits me very much, as I mentioned before. It is a simple life, and, when once certain hardships are conquered, it is very pleasant. I like it! I get plenty of bathing – the sea is wonderfully warm – plenty of fresh air. In my spare time I write, play chess with George, read, or study a book on bridge (Culbertsons) with George, whom I met on ship and who has stuck with me ever since. Together we have had a great deal of fun, and now we are on a wireless truck together.

I wish Douglas every piece of good luck in the Cadet Corps – and I hope he is pleased with the stamps. I am sending him through Edna. As before, I feel Ken should stay put. Give them both my love – I think of you all a great deal.

Love

Gordon

**MILITARY AIRGRAPH SERVICE AUTHORISED BY EGYPTIAN
POSTAL ADMINISTRATION**

To Mrs H. Huntington

Sender's Address:
SGM Huntington 2575957
Signals 68th Heavy A.A. Regt.
M.E.F.

10th June 1942

My dear Mother,

This is a challenge to you! Can you manage it? Can you write a legible airgraph! I doubt it.

I am still very well, and quite pleased now that mail is coming through.

Should you not hear from me regularly at any time I don't want you to worry dear because there are many factors to be taken into account with mail. The service is good but not infallible. I shall write at least once a week to you anyway.

Now, starting from JUNE 15th my voluntary allotment will be 2/6 per day. You will not get confirmation of this until later on, when you should draw a retrospective amount from that date. Now that I have received your cabled amount I will not need pay – I doubt if I shall even call upon that.

Well Mother I send you fondest love, take care of yourself dear. Please remember me to Kenny and Douglas.

Cheerio for now

Gordon

MILITARY AIRGRAPH SERVICE AUTHORISED BY EGYPTIAN POSTAL ADMINISTRATION

To K. Huntington Esq.

Sender's Address:
SGM Huntington 2575957
Signals 68th Heavy A.A. Regt.
M.E.F.

12th June 1942

Dear Ken,

I hear from Dad that you are finding things a little easier with your work nowadays. I am glad to hear of it because you have had a long spell of work with little time off. I wonder what you get up to on your day off? I expect you brush your hair nearly off your head, put on my best suit and go out with your latest girl friend!

Tell Douglas that I am doing my best to get as many foreign stamps as possible – the bulk of them should arrive in August by surface mail. I hear he has joined the Air Cadets? At what age do they take boys for that then?

If you get time write and let me know what you are doing and how you like it. Give my love to all at home.

"An iznak lahja" – which means "See you soon" or "Don't forget the money you owe me".

Love

Gordon

CABLE AND WIRELESS TELEGRAM LIMITED
"Via Imperial"
**The first line of this telegram shows:- Number, office of origin, date.
(NOTE: Sansorigine is used to denote that the office of origin has been suppressed.)**

Dated 18 June '42
Received 24 June '42

SANS ORIGINE

To Mrs Huntington, 23 Crichton Ave, Wallington, Surrey

LETTERS RECEIVED MANY THANKS

PLEASE DONT WORRY

LOVE

GORDON HUNTINGTON

Letter from Army Record Office Royal Corps of Signals.

No. *CAS/M/02063*   Army Form B. 104 - 83

To Mr Huntington
Stamped 29 July 1942

Sir,

I regret to have to inform you that a report has been received from the War Office to the effect that (No.) *2575957* (Rank) *Sigmn* (Name) *HUNTINGTON, Gordon, Harold* (Regiment) ROYAL CORPS OF SIGNALS was posted as "missing" on the *20/6/42*

The report that he is missing does not necessarily mean that he has been killed, as he may be a prisoner of war or temporarily separated from his regiment.

Official reports that men are prisoners of war take some time to reach this country, and if he has been captured by the enemy it is probable that unofficial news will reach you first. In that case I am to ask you to forward any postcard or letter received at once to this Office, and it will be returned to you as soon as possible.

Should any further official information be received it will be at once communicated to you.

I am,
Sir,
Your obedient Servant

Signature Capt
For Officer in charge of Records.

IMPORTANT.
Any change of your address should be immediately notified to this Office.

ADVICE TO THE RELATIVE OF A MAN WHO IS MISSING

In view of the official notification that your relative is missing, you will naturally wish to hear what is being done to trace him.

The Service Departments make every endeavour to discover the fate of missing men, and draw upon all likely sources of information about them.

A man who is missing after an engagement may possibly be a Prisoner of War. Continuous efforts are made to speed up the machinery whereby the names and camp addresses of Prisoners of War can reach this Country. The official means is by lists of names prepared by the enemy Government. These lists take some time to compile, especially if there is a long journey from the place of capture to a Prisoners of War camp. Consequently "capture cards" filled in by the Prisoners themselves soon after capture and sent home to their relatives are often the first news received in this Country that a man is a Prisoner of War. That is why you are asked in the accompanying letter to forward at once any card or letter you may receive, if it is the first news you have had.

Even if no news is received that a missing man is a Prisoner of War, endeavours to trace him do not cease. Enquiries are pursued not only among those who were serving with him, but also through diplomatic channels and the International Red Cross Committee at Geneva.

The moment reliable news is obtained from any of these sources it is sent to the Service Department concerned. They will pass the news on to you at once, if they are satisfied that it is reliable. It would be cruel to raise false hopes, such as may well be raised if you listen to one other possible channel of news, namely, the enemy's broadcasts. These are listened to by official listeners, working continuously night and day. The few names of Prisoners given by enemy announcers are carefully checked. They are often misleading, and this is not surprising, for the object of the inclusion of Prisoners' names in these broadcasts is not to help the relatives of Prisoners, but to induce British listeners to hear some tale which otherwise they could not be made to hear. The only advantage of listening to these broadcasts is an advantage to the enemy.

The official listeners can never miss any name included in an enemy broadcast. They pass every name on to the Service Department concerned. There every name is checked, and in every case where a name can be verified, the news is sent direct to the relatives.

There is, therefore, a complete official service designed to secure for you and to tell you all discoverable news about your relative. This official service is also a very human service, which well understands the anxiety of relatives and will spare no effort to relieve it.

CAS/M/02063

Royal Signals Records Office,
Balmore House,
Caversham,
READING.

Dated 29.8.42
(Received 31st August 1942)

Dear Sir,

No. 2575957 SIGMN. HUNTINGTON G.H.

I regret it is my duty to inform you that the name of your *son*, the above mentioned soldier, was included in a recent Broadcast emanating from enemy sources as having been taken Prisoner in the recent fighting in North Africa.

This information may have reached you from some other quarter and I hasten to inform you that this notification for the present can only be treated as unconfirmed.

If your *son* has had the misfortune to fall into the hands of the enemy, you will next hear from him direct on a capture card and at a later date when concentration is completed will receive his Camp address when you will be able to write. Should you hear further, please advise me at once and I should be grateful for sight of the message you receive for verification and return and needless to say any further information that reaches this office will be transmitted to you without delay.

Yours faithfully

Signature Lieut.
for O i/c R. Signals Records.

Hand written undated note in ink from the Vatican War Enquiry Department.

Vatican War Enquiry Dept.,
11 Cavendish Square
London, W1

Tel: Langham 1215

Vatican Crest

Apostolic Delegation

Dear Mr Huntington,

Thank you for your note. We will send all the information you have given us to the Vatican at once. I hope before long we may get news of your son. I am glad to say we have often been most successful in tracing the missing.

I remain,

Yours most sincerely,

P.P. Signature

WAR ORGANISATION
of the
BRITISH RED CROSS SOCIETY and ORDER
OF ST. JOHN OF JERUSALEM

PRISONERS OF WAR DEPARTMENT

H. Huntington, Esq.,   ST. JAME'S PALACE,
23, Crichton, Avenue,   London, S.W. 1
Wallington,
Surrey.

                                                            8th Oct, 1942

Dear Mr Huntington,

                           Sgmn. G.H. Huntington

    We are glad to hear that your son has been reported a prisoner of war, although up to the present we have not received official confirmation of this.

    We are, however, sending you a copy of our circular PW/99B/42, which gives full instructions about letters for prisoners of war, which for the time being you should address as shown in paragraph 2b.

    If you hear direct from the prisoner, or receive official confirmation before hearing from us again, please let us know so that we can then advise you again about addressing your letters and about the despatch of parcels.

                                          Yours sincerely,
                                          Pp E.M. THORNTON. *B.M.G.*
                                          Director.

PW/99B/42

WAR ORGANISATION
of the
BRITISH RED CROSS SOCIETY and ORDER OF ST. JOHN OF JERSUALEM.

PRISONERS OF WAR DEPARTMENT,
St. James's Palace, London, S.W.1.

May, 1942

INFORMATION ABOUT LETTERS FOR PRISONERS OF WAR IN GERMAN AND ITALIAN HANDS.

1. (a) There is no limit to the number of letters that may be written to Prisoners of War, but it is well to remember that, as they all have to pass through two censorships, the greater the number sent, the greater may be the delay in delivery.

   (b) Letters should be written as clearly as possible, should deal with personal matters only, and should not exceed both sides of one sheet of notepaper. The writer's name and address must be written on the back of the envelope, but if the writer is serving in His Majesty's Forces, the name and address of the unit must not be given, but a private address substituted. The name and camp address of the Prisoner should be written on the letter as well as on the envelope. The most recent address sent by the Prisoner should be carefully copied.

   (c) Letters to Prisoners of War may either be sent post free by the ordinary Prisoners of War Post, which means that they are conveyed by sea to Lisbon and from there to Germany or Italy by air-mail; or all the way from Great Britain by air, in which case they should be marked "By Air Mail", and require a 5d. stamp. Letters should be posted in the ordinary way and not be sent to the Red Cross to be forwarded. A special air letter-card for use in communicating with British Prisoners of War and interned civilians in German or Italian hands is now obtainable at the principal Post Offices. The cards cost 3d. each and, posted in the ordinary way, will be forwarded to Prisoners of War (see paragraph 2(b) below) and to Prisoners interned in neutral European countries.

2.   <u>Letters to Prisoners of War in Germany.</u>

(a) Letters to Prisoners of War in Germany, <u>if both the camp address and Prisoner of War number are known</u>, should be addressed as follows:-

PRISONERS OF WAR POST
KRIEGSGEFANGENENPOST
      Rank.   Name.
      British Prisoner of War No..........
      Name and Number of Camp,
      Germany.

Prisoners of War in Germany write their letters on printed forms or cards supplied by the German authorities. The Prisoner of War number and the camp address will be found on the back of the letter or card after the words "Gefangenennummer" and "Lager-Bezeichnung". Place names should not be included in the address unless they are given by the Prisoner as part of his address.

Notes:-

(1) If the camp address is known, but not the Prisoner of War number, letters may be addressed as shown in paragraph 2 (a) above, but the Service number should be given before the rank and name.

(2) R.A.F. Prisoners of War in Dulag Luft, Germany, are not given Prisoner of War numbers, and the address on letters sent direct to the camp should, therefore, include the Service number before the rank and name.

(b) If the Camp address is not known, the service number should be included, and the letter addressed as follows:-

PRISONERS OF WAR POST
KRIEGSGEFANGENENPOST
Service No.   Rank.   Name.
British Prisoner of War,
c/o Agence Centrale des Prisonniers de Guerre,
Geneva.

3.   Letters to Prisoners of War in Italy

(a). Letters to Prisoners of War in Italy should be
     addressed as follows:-

PRISONERS OF WAR POST
SERVICE DES PRISONNIERS DE GUERRE
     Service No.   Rank.   Name.
        British Prisoner of War,
           Campo P.G. (Number)
             Posta Militare (Number)
               Italy.

The most recent address sent by the Prisoner should be carefully copied. The numbers after the letters "P.G." and "P.M." (Posta Militare) form part of the camp address and should not be confused with the "Prisoner of War numbers" which are given to Prisoners in Germany, but up to the present not generally to those in Italian hands.

(b) If a Prisoner is known to be in Italian hands, but his camp address has not yet been received, letters may be addressed as follows:-

PRISONERS OF WAR POST
SERVICE DES PRISONNIERS DE GUERRE
Service No.   Rank. Name.
    British Prisoner of War,
       c/o Croce Rossa Italiana,
         Via Puglie 6,
         Rome.

4. Enclosures.
    Unmounted photographs or snapshots of a purely personal nature may be enclosed in letters to Prisoners of War, but no other pictures or printed matter of any kind. Any enclosure may cause the letter to be delayed for special examination. The name and address of the Prisoner and of the sender should be written on the back of photographs, etc.

5. Enquiries and Messages by Telegram.
    The regulations of the censor do not permit telegrams to be sent direct to Prisoners of War, but in urgent cases the Prisoners of War Department will send by telegraph to the International Red Cross Committee at Geneva, an enquiry or a message for a Prisoner. These messages are forwarded by post from Geneva, except in very urgent circumstances, when they are sent by telegraph.

BRITISH RED CROSS SOCIETY and ORDER of St. JOHN of JERUSALEM
JOINT WAR COMMITTEE (SURREY)

Prisoners of War Department

Deputy Chairman
MISS N. KING-CHURCH

August, 1942.

The Surrey Red Cross and St. John Joint War Committee, Prisoners of War Department, has organised a scheme to help to provide goods for the three monthly next-of-kin parcels allowed to be sent to the Prisoner by his own relatives. Where the family is unable to meet the whole expense of sending a really good parcel of comforts, the Red Cross and St. John Organisation or other Societies concerned will help with extra gifts.

They will also undertake, if next-of-kin wish, to pack and send off to Finsbury Circus next-of-kin parcels, the material for which is supplied by relatives, and so ensure that the parcel contains only those things which may be sent, and that Forms and labels are filled in correctly.

Please reply on the enclosed postcard, and if help or advice is needed, a Visitor will be sent to see you, or you will be told the address of the local organisation. Please note that the enclosed card only needs a 1d stamp.

Signature
Chairman, Prisoners of War Department.

Card received with covering letter 22/10/42

WAR ORGANISATION of the BRITISH RED CROSS SOCIETY and ORDER OF ST. JOHN OF JERUSALEM

WOUNDED, MISSING AND RELATIVES DEPARTMENT

7 Belgrave Square
London, SW1

Re: Sigm G. H. Huntington – 2575957 – R. Signals

11.9.42

Dear *Mr Huntington,*

We have received your letter of *2.9.42* in which you tell us that you have information that your son's name has been broadcast as a prisoner of war. We have been in communication with the B.B.C. and have verified that the news was given out from *The Vatican* on *24.8.42.*

As broadcasts from foreign stations are not always entirely reliable we fear that this news cannot be taken as official, but in this case as the particulars given were correct we think you have every reason to hope that it is true.

We are very glad that you have had this good news and sincerely hope that you will soon receive an official notification confirming that your *son* is a prisoner of war.

Yours sincerely,
Margaret Ampthill p.p.

Camp Benghazi
No address given in broadcast.

Abbey 5841 Extn 25 (Interview Room)

P.T.O.

Will you communicate with our Prisoners of War Dept., St. James Palace, SW1.
You will [be] given whatever information is available & you will be told how letters & parcels should be sent.

3rd Air mail letter card P.O.
Rank & Name

C/o Croce Rossa Italiana
Via Puglii No 6
Rome

BRITISH RED CROSS SOCIETY.

SURREY BRANCH.
BEDDINGTON & WALLINGTON DIVISION

25th October 1942

Dear Mr Huntington,

Sglmn. G. H. Huntington, No.2575957. Royal Corpos of Signals

I have to-day been informed by my Headquarters of the fact that your son is a Prisoner of War.

If at any time you are in need of help or advice in connection with parcels to your son, or any other matter, no matter how small, I hope you will not hesitate to get in touch with me, when I shall do my best to be of any help I can.

Yours sincerely,
Mrs F. Ashton
Divisional Secretary

No. *Cas/P/02063*   Army Form B. 104-83A.

ARMY RECORD OFFICE
Royal Corps of Signals

Stamped 2 Nov 1942

Sir,

    I have to inform you that a report has been received from the War Office to the effect that (No.) *2575957* (Rank) *Sigmn* (Name) *Huntington G. H.* (Regiment) ROYAL CORPS OF SIGNALS is a Prisoner of War *present address not yet known.*

    Should any other information be received concerning him, such information will be at once communicated to you.

    Instructions as to the method of communicating with Prisoners of War can be obtained at any Post Office.

I am,

Sir,

Your obedient Servant,

Signature Capt

for Officer in charge of Records.

"General Enquiries about prisoners of war and the treatment to which they are entitled may be made, either in person or by letter, at the Prisoner of War Enquiry Centre, Curzon Street House, Curzon Street London, W.I. (open 10 a.m. – 6 p.m. Monday to Friday; 10 a.m. to 1 p.m. Saturdays.)"

Cas/P/02063/27039

Royal Signals Record Office,
Balmore House,
Caversham, READING.

To Mrs Huntington
23, Crichton Avenue,
Wallington,
Surrey

16th November 1942

Dear Madam,

<u>Re. 2575957 Sigmn. Huntington G.H.</u>

A report has been received here per the war office stating that during a recent broadcast emanating from enemy sources a message from your son was received.

Should you have missed this broadcast, I feel sure that you would like the message which reads as follows:-

"Sigmn. Gordon Harold Huntington to Mrs Huntington,.....Wallington, Surrey. Telephone .... Both Safe and well, love Gordon."

We have received no news as to what camp he is in, but as soon as further information reaches this office you will be notified at once.

Yours faithfully,

O Anderson

Capt.
for O i/c R.Signals Records.

From George R. Oliver,
1, Hartley-avenue, E.6.

28th November, 1942

The following was received over the German-controlled wireless
from Calais at 8.55 p.m. Nov. 27, 1942:-

2575957 Signalman Gordon Harold Huntington,
To Mrs Edith Huntington,
23 Crichton-avenue,
Wallington, Surrey:

Message: Telephone Fishel Anfield 388 Liverpool. Both well.
Love.

_____

Fishel Anfield 388 Liverpool
My prisoner sons message enemy broadcast
27 Nov telephone Fishel both well
Huntington
23 C.A.
Wallington Surrey

BRITISH RED CROSS SOCIETY

SURREY BRANCH.
BEDDINGTON & WALLINGTON DIVISION

To H. Huntington Esq,
23 Creighton Avenue.
Wallington.

30.11.42.

Dear Sir,

The Vice-President has asked me to acknowledge your generous donation of £1.1.0. to our Prisoners of War Fund.

The parcels of food sent out by the Red Cross are, I know, greatly appreciated by Prisoners of War and your kindness will enable us to carry on with this good work. Please accept our grateful thanks.

Yours sincerely,

Mrs. F. Ashton
Divisional Secretary

WAR ORGANISATION
of the
BRITISH RED CROSS SOCIETY and ORDER
OF ST. JOHN OF JERUSALEM

WOUNDED, MISSING AND RELATIVES
DEPARTMENT

December 2nd 1942

Dear Mrs Huntington,

The following message has been broadcast by the wireless from:

Sgn. Gordon Harold Huntington, 2575957, on Calais Radio, 27/11/1942:-

"Telephone ?Fishell, Anfield 388, Liverpool; both safe, well. Love from Gordon."

To: Mrs Edith Huntington, 23 Crichton Avenue, Wellington, Surrey.

We are so pleased to be able to send you this, as if you have not already received it from other sources, we feel sure that this personal communication may do much to allay your anxiety.

Yours sincerely,

Margaret Ampthill
Chairman.
Pp Kb

Letter from Cecil Fishel's father to my parents' address.

FISHEL BROS. & CO.
Woollen Warehousemen.

WOLLEN DEPARTMENT

2nd Dec 1942

Dear Sir or Madam,

I received a telegram stating that "My prisoner sons message enemy broadcast 27th November telephone Fishel both well. Huntington 23. Crichton Avenue Wallington Surrey."

I should be glad if you could possibly favour me with any particulars as to the origin of the broadcast message. If this means your sons message was to say he and my son are both well permit me of offer my heartfelt thanks and the heartiest congratulations to you on this good news. My son has been missing since 20th June Middle East forces and have not received any word from him since he has been taken prisoner and your telegram has relieved a great deal of the mental anguish that I have borne since. I am indeed grateful to you and await your reply.

Yours faithfully,

D Fishel

My sons name and number is
Signalman C.L. FISHEL 2439674
Royal Signal Corp.
M.E.F.

Cas/P/02063

R. Signals Records Office,
Balmore House,
Caversham,
Reading.

7th December, 1942

Mrs Huntington
23 Critchton Avenue
Wallington.
Surrey.
_____

Dear Madam,

<u>Re No.2575957 Sigmn Huntington G.H.</u>

A report has been received here per the War Office stating that during a recent broadcast emanating from enemy sources a message from your son, the above named, was received.

Should you have missed this broadcast I feel sure that you would like to have the message which reads as follows:- "Sigmn. Gordon Harold Huntington No.2575957 to Mrs Huntington, 23 Critchton Avenue, Wallington, Surrey. Telephone (?Fishell) Anfield 388, Liverpool. Both safe and well. Love from Gordon.

It is believed that the name mentioned in this message refers to No.2349674 Sigmn. Fishel. Cecil Leon who is recorded as a Prisoner of War in this office.

Yours faithfully,
Signature

for O.i/c R.Signals Records.

PMH

ROYAL SIGNALS ASSOCIATION,
44, Princess Gardens,
London, S.W. 7.

8/12/42
(Acknowledged 21/12/42)

Ref. 3063

Dear *Mrs Huntingdon*

We write to you as next of kin of *Sigmn G.H. Huntingdon* whom we are informed is reported to be a Prisoner of War. As soon as you know his camp address you should inform the Red Cross who will send you the necessary coupons, label and instructions enabling you to send him a parcel of clothing and comforts.

It is realised that in these days it may be difficult in some places to get the permitted items. The Signals Association has, at present, a supply of most of the things allowed to be sent and will be glad to help in any way possible. If you find it difficult to make up your parcel it is suggested that you send the label, unused coupons etc. to us at the above address together with such items as you may be able to collect for your parcel. At the same time would you please tell us if your Prisoner of War has any special requirements giving us his sizes and measurements together with his full camp address. The Association would then complete the parcel and hand it over to the Red Cross for despatch (owing to Board of Trade regulations we are not able to send these articles to the next of kin to put in the parcels themselves).

If you have not already heard from your Prisoner of War it is so hoped that you will have news in the near future.

Yours truly,
ANNE CLEMENTI SMITH
Hon. Secretary.

VATICAN WAR ENQUIRY DEPT.
11 Cavendish Square,
London, W.1

Vatican Crest

SECRETARIAT OF STATE
TO HIS HOLINESS

Written 19/12/42
Received 29/3/43

The Apostolic Delegate has much pleasure in sending the enclosed message to you. The message was collected by a Representative sent by His Holiness the Pope to visit Prisoner of War Camps in Italy.

Sender Gordon Huntington
Rank Signalman
No. 2575957
Camp no. Transit Camp 85
Military Post P.M.3450
Addressee Mrs Huntington H.

Wishing you a happy Christmas and a prosperous New Year.

POST CARD for war prisoners
Cartolina Postale per Prigionieri di Guerra

To Mr & Mrs H Huntington
From Huntington, Gordon Harold, Signalman, Royal Signals
Date as postmark

My dear, *Parents & Edna*

I am alright (I have not been wounded). I am a prisoner of the Italians and I am being treated well.

Shortly I shall be transferred to a prisoner's camp and I will let you have my new address.

Only then I will be able to receive letters from you and to reply. With love,

Gordon   (signature) *Gordon Huntington*

Posta di prigioniero di Guerra to Mrs H Huntington

From Huntington, Gordon Harold, Signalman 2575957
Transit Campo 85 PM 3450 Italia

Stamped 22 Dec 1942
Received 16/4/43

Mother dear. This is my first opportunity of writing to you since being captured on June 21st and I want to assure you that I am quite all right and you have nothing to fear. My only trouble has been the thought that you and Edna and Dad have been starved of news from me for so long. But it was unavoidable. I always have said that no news is good news, and I hope that you have believed in that also dear. Now you may write as often as you like and send me parcels (refer Post Office instructions). In fact I will now be a thorough nuisance because I want you to try and send me chocolate, cigarettes, pack of cards, book on Italian grammar, handkerchiefs and towel. I hope you are still well dear, and that Dad and the boys are fit also. At the moment there is only this card available but I hope for more, the next one I will write to Edna. I do hope that she is safe and well, please give her all my love. All of you at home – the lads, Auntie Hilda and Grandma, Edna and her dear Mother – I wish you all safe keeping during 1943. Very soon we shall be together again and I will chew a pipe over many a tale like the old campaigner that I am! Goodbye for now dear. My love to both of you and the boys. Gordon

CAS/P/02063/27093

H. Huntington Esq.,   Royal Signals Records Office.
23, Crichton Avenue.   Balmore House.
Wallington,   Caversham,
SURREY.   READING.

Dear Sir,   6th January 1943.

<u>No. 2075957 Sigmn. G.H. Huntington.</u>

I have to thank you for your letter of 30th December enclosing the Card received from your Son which I now return to you.

The account of your communications with the Vatican War Enquiry Department is indeed interesting and I am inclined to think that the inference you have drawn with regard to your Son's present location is probably the correct one.

For your information, the recent reports we have received concerning your Son may be tabulated as follows –

Reported "missing"   20.6.1942
Prisoner of War "unconfirmed", report received from
Vatican City   24.8.1942
Reported Prisoner of War on International Red Cross
Society's Telegram   November 1942
Received Radio Message from Rome   10.11.1942
Received Radio Message from Calais   27.11.1942

I sincerely hope you may continue to hear from your Son and that the time may not be too distant when he will be restored to you.

Yours faithfully,

O. Anderson
Capt., R. Signals.
for O i/c R. Signals Records

IJC.

Letter I wrote to my parents where I mention "Jane" but this time I do not use it as a ruse to inform them of my whereabouts.

Posta di prigioniero di Guerra to Mr & Mrs H Huntington

From Huntington, Gordon Harold, Signalman 2575957
Transit Campo 85 PM 3450 Italia

Stamped 7 Jan 1943
Received 8/5/43

Dear Mother and Dad, I expect you have received one letter from me by now, telling you what little news I could in the space provided. I hope you are all OK at home. I have also written twice to Edna asking her for certain things, but I want you to send them of course, as you will receive certain privileges from organisations at home. If you cannot send an Italian grammar book then please send my HG Wells short stories, for reading is my main pastime. Of course I can give you little news, but I am well and comfortable. The Red Cross does everything possible to help us, sending a parcel once a fortnight and 5 cigs each day. These things that I ask for in my letters to you and Edna are simply to give you an idea of articles necessary but at the moment lacking! You may be unable to send them, in which case I will quite understand. Please write Paymaster Signals Reading informing my safety and remind them of my third years' increment of 9d per day, also enquire conditions of pay to prisoners of war. At the moment we are all awaiting the Red Cross Christmas parcel, which I believe is good! Also letters from home! I hope that everything is all right with you, is Mother OK? I want to have a little heart to heart talk with you soon. I now appreciate all you have done for me in the past. It has taken this to show it to me. Well, I would like a little news of Jane if you can find space, Dad. Until my next letter, love to you all, keep well. Gordon

Poste Italiane Cartolina Postale Per Prigionieri Di Guerra to Mrs H Huntington

From Huntington, Gordon Harold, Signalman 2575957
Campo Transit 85 PM 3450 Italia

Stamped 10 JAN 1943
Received 8/2/43

Dear Mother. In case you should receive this before my other letters, I am quite safe and well. I wish you all a Happy 1943 and trust we will all be together again before the finish of it. Please give my love to Dad and the boys – letters should be regular now. Hope you are all well dear. Gordon

FISHEL BROS. & CO.

Woollen Warehousemen.

WOLLEN DEPARTMENT

11ᵗʰ January 1943

Dear Mr & Mrs Huntington

I have just received a letter from my son, Cecil in which he says that he is well and in good health. His address is now

FISHEL. CECIL. LEON
SIGNALMAN 2349674, P.G. No 68. PM 3300. ITALIA.
HUT 2

I do sincerely hope you have by now received the same good news of your "Gordon" if so would esteem it a favour if you will let me have his address so that I could write to him. It would be nice if the boys (Cecil & Gordon) were in the same camp. Thanking you once again for your great kindness in sending telegram and letter. Wishing you all that is brightest and best.

Yours very sincerely

D Fishel

AM/76301.

PW/144A/42.

WAR ORGANISATION
of the
BRITISH RED CROSS SOCIETY and ORDER OF ST. JOHN OF JERUSALEM

PRISONERS OF WAR DEPARTMENT

11th February 1943

Dear **Mrs Huntington,**

<u>Sgmn.G.H.Huntington</u>

We are very glad that your **son's** camp address is now known. Letters and parcels should now be addressed to him as follows:-

PRISONERS OF WAR POST

SERVICE DES PRISONNIERS DE GUERRE

2575957 Sgmn. G.H.Huntington,

British Prisoner of War,

Campo P.G., **85**

Posta Militare, **3450.**

Italy.

We hope that our leaflets will give you all the information you require, but we shall always be glad to help you in any way possible.

Yours sincerely,

pp E.M. Thornton. *P.Q.R.*

Director.

Poste Italiane Cartolina Postale Per Prigion-ieri Di Guerra to Mr & Mrs H Huntington

From Huntington, Gordon Harold, Signalman 2575957
Campo Transit 85 PM 3450 Italia

Stamped 24 FEB 1943

Dear Mother & Dad, I am receiving letters now fairly often from you, and now you have my address it is all right for letters and parcels to be sent to me regularly. Have you tried Rowntrees or Cadburys for parcels for prisoners-of-war? Wishing you all the best & I send you my love, and to Edna. Gordon.

Posta di prigioniero di Guerra to Mr & Mrs H Huntington

From Huntington, Gordon Harold, Signalman 2575957

Transit Campo 85 PM 3450 Italia
Written 6/3/43
Received 6/8/43

Dear Dad and Mother. So far I have received 17 letters from you and Edna – the best record of the bungalow I believe. I consider myself the luckiest in the group for mail. We are divided into groups of 100 to a bungalow in this camp, but it doesn't look as if I shall be working on farms or anywhere, as they don't take Imperial troops. However – I shall be home soon! The dates of your letters are 6 & 17 Aug, 15 & 24 Sept, & 10 & 22 Oct, 5 & 18 November in case you should be keeping a check on mail. I am immensely relieved to hear that Mother is OK now, and looking after the chicks – it must have been a great anxiety to hear nothing for so long. Edna tells me that Mother has been very kind to her and I'm so glad. Regarding Dad's bout with Newman – I knew he wouldn't lose in the end. I am curious to know more – are you hand-in-glove with Newman now, Dad? I was pleased to hear, also, that the Evening News published my name. It looks as if the service for P.O.W. is as efficient as possible under the circumstances – we now get a Red X parcel once a week, and we are expecting clothing parcels shortly. I have mentioned my needs previously to you – any of my clothing will be acceptable, shoes, socks – anything! And chocolate! Tell Mother not to worry now, give her my love and remember me to the boys Ken & Douglas. Also give my love to Hilda & Vandy, Grandma & Grandpa. Gordon

Poste Italiane Cartolina Postale Per Prigionieri Di Guerra to Mr & Mrs H Huntington

From Huntington, Gordon Harold, Signalman 2575957
Transit 85 PM 3450 Italia

Stamped 31 MAR1943
Received 20/8/43

My dear Mother & Father. I have so far received all your letters up to February last month. I am quite OK and almost fit again. It is a pity that I cannot tell you & Edna my experiences but I shall be able to do so soon. I am glad to hear that Ken is in the RASC, and that Douglas is doing his best. All my love to you. Gordon

VATICAN WAR ENQUIRY DEPT.
11 Cavendish Square, London, W.1

The enclosed message was collected by a representative of His Holiness the Pope and is forwarded to you on behalf of His Holiness by Archbishop Godfrey, the Apostolic Delegate in Great Britain.

N.B. – Any correspondence relative to this message should be sent to the above address and stamped with a 2½ d. stamp.

Vatican Crest

SECRETARIAT OF STATE TO HIS HOLINESS

Easter 1943

Sender Huntington Gordon Harold
Rank Signalman
No. 2575957
Camp No. 85 PM3450

Addressee Mrs H Huntington

Message (25 words)

My love to you all, take care of Edna

Poste Italiane Cartolina Postale Per Prigionieri Di Guerra to Master D.H. Huntington

From Huntington, Gordon Harold, Signalman 2575957
Campo 85 PM 3450 Italia

Stamped 20 APR 1943
Received 24/5/43

Dear Douglas, Here's a note to tell you that I'm quite OK but cursing my luck. I expect you think I'm some sort of chap to walk straight in with my hands up! I hear that you are getting tall now – keep it up too. I hope you got the stamps I sent you from the desert. Much love, Gordon

WAR ORGANISATION
of the
BRITISH RED CROSS SOCIETY and ORDER OF ST. JOHN OF JERUSALEM

PRISONERS OF WAR DEPARTMENT

THE NEW BODLEIAN.

OXFORD.

22nd April 1943

Dear Sir,

In reply to your enquiry books to Prisoners of War can be sent through any bookseller holding the requisite export permit.

We generally recommend either of the following Italian Grammars:

Wilkins: First Italian Book Harrap	3/6
Perini: Conversation Grammar	7/6
Hachette Key	6/6

We can however not say whether the Perini is available at present. It would be best if you consulted your bookseller as to what books he has in stock.

Should you however have difficulties in procuring the book, please let us know, and we shall be glad to order an Italian Grammar through our bookseller.

We would notify you of the cost of the book when we receive the invoice from our booksellers, which would not be for some weeks after the book had been ordered.

If you wish us to obtain the book would you please let us have your son's name, rank, service number and full camp address, quoting these particulars in any further correspondence.

If your son wants a dictionary we would suggest Hugo's Italian Dictionary (3/6). He could also be sent an Italian Reader, but these are very difficult to obtain.

Yours faithfully,
E. Herdman
(E. Herdman)

Handwritten note to indicate both Perini books "Sent off, with Hugo Dictionary, from *Hachettes 27.4.43*.

Poste Italiane Cartolina Postale Per Prigionieri Di Guerra to Mrs Huntington

From Huntington, Gordon Harold, Signalman 2575957
Campo 85 PM 3450 Italia

Stamped 24 APR 1943
Received 23/8/43

My dear Mother. I hope you are getting my letters all right – we are allowed one card and one letter a week and I try to write you something every time. I am now back to normal health again, but I badly want some toilet materials. My love to all dear. Gordon

Poste Italiane Cartolina Postale Per Prigionieri Di Guerra to H Huntington Esq.

From Huntington, Gordon Harold, Signalman 2575957
Campo 85 PM 3450 Italia

Stamped 9 MAY 1943
Received 2/9/43

Dear Dad, Yesterday a large consignment of mail arrived here and, when they have sorted it out, I expect to receive some recent mail from you. You can safely address parcels to this address. I am looking forward to toilet material and some books. Played five games of soccer in two days! Keeping fit now. Gordon

Letter from Regimental Paymaster, written in pen and ink.

MEMORANDUM.

From: REGTL. PAYMASTER, R. SIGS. READING
To: Mr H. Huntington
Sender's Reference *RCS/NE/POW.*
Date *17.5.43*

<u>2575957 Sgm. Huntington. G.H.</u>

Dear Sir,

*With reference to your letter of the 11th inst., you are informed that your son's army pay, has been and will be credited to his army pay account, for the period that he is a prisoner of war, **plus any increments due.***

It is regretted that no further details regarding your son's pay can be given you, as under existing army regulations, this information can only be given direct to the soldier.

If you will forward your son's prison camp address to this office, a statement of his account will be sent to him.

Yours faithfully,
Signature Lieut
for REGTL. PAYMASTER,
R. SIGS. READING

(Answered 19.5.43)

Posta di prigioniero di Guerra to Mr & Mrs H Huntington

From Huntington, Gordon Harold, Signalman 2575957
Campo 85 PM 3450 Italia

Stamped 19/5/43

My dear Mother & Father. I have had an almost regular mail from Dad for the last two months – but of course I know that he writes for you both. I am anxious to know if Mother is all right, and not worrying about little Wandering Willy. Do you realise that when I get back I shall be thinking of getting married? Do you? Can you imagine what a job Edna will have! Clothing will be expensive won't it? So you had better tell Douglas not to sit down too much in those suits of mine, and to go the quickest way to everywhere because of the leather he might waste otherwise. I'm feeling quite bright today – it must be all the macaroni that I don't get. Do you know that our friends have started making boots out of leather owing to the shortage of cardboard? Well that's about enough of the fooling – both of you. You can tell for yourself that I'm as offensive as ever! I think of you all very much, and I'm so glad that everything is OK. Gordon

Poste Italiane Cartolina Postale Per Prigionieri Di Guerra to Mr & Mrs Huntington

From Huntington, Gordon Harold, Signalman 2575957
85 PM 3450 Italia

Stamped 30th MAY1943
Received 21/9/43

My dear Mother & Father, My birthday tomorrow! It doesn't seem all that time ago that I left home. We have been issued with shirts, vests, socks & boots now, but we all await personal parcels and cigarette parcels – only a few having received them to date. All my love to you Gordon

Poste Italiane Cartolina Postale Per Prigionieri Di Guerra to Mr & Mrs Huntington

From Huntington, Gordon Harold, Signalman 2575957
Campo 70 PM 3300 (No 2 Compound) Italia

Written 12/6/43

My dear Mother & Father, Well this is my new address – please send all future mail & parcels to Camp 70. Incidentally my second personal parcel will probably reach me before the first, owing to the move. I have had a letter from Grandpa, two from Betty – the one from Grandpa was lucky to reach me! All my love to you. Gordon

Posta di prigioniero di Guerra to
Mrs E Huntington

From Huntington, Gordon Harold, Signalman 2575957
Campo 70 PM 3300 Italia

Written 13/7/43

My dear Mother – I have managed to obtain ink for this letter because it concerns my army pay. A week before capture I authorised an allotment of an additional 1/6d per day to you w.e.f. 15/6/42. If this allotment has not been effected then it makes no difference because I now give you full authority to withdraw all my pay and credits to the date of receipt of this letter, and to continue to withdraw my pay each week until further notice. In other words I want you to place my money in a banking a/c or to buy savings certificates with it, as it gains no interest with the Army. I prefer certificates. I was taken prisoner on the 21st June 1942. Since then – when my pay was 4/- per day including your allotment of 2/6 per day – I should receive another 9d p.d. for 3 years war service, and any increases of pay made to soldiers since by act of Parliament. I have written to the Regimental Paymaster, Royal Signals, Reading telling him of this letter.

Well dear I am quite all right, but worried about you. No parcels received yet from you or anyone and lately no mail. Give my love to Dad & the boys – also give Edna a kiss from me. G.H. Huntington

Poste Italiane Cartolina Postale Per Prigionieri Di Guerra to Mrs Huntington

From Huntington, Gordon Harold, Signalman 2575957
Campo 70 PM 3300 Italia

Written 13/7/43
Received 2/9/43

My dear Mother. I have not had any mail lately and so far no parcels have arrived at all but that is my smallest worry. All I want to know is whether you are all safe and well – I am fine myself dear. Give my love to Dad & the boys. Tell Edna that I write once a week and have done since October. Gordon

---

CAS/P/02063

Mr H. Huntington,
23 Crichton Avenue,
Wallington, Surrey.

Royal Signals Records Office.
Balmore House.
Caversham,
READING.

27th July 1943

Dear *Sir,*

<u>Re No. *2575957 Sigmn HUNTINGTON G.H.*</u>

I have to acknowledge receipt of your letter of recent date concerning the Camp address of the above –named soldier.

I thank you for the information given which has been duly noted in our records.

Yours faithfully,

Signature
for O i/c R. Signals Records

Poste Italiane Cartolina Postale Per Prigionieri Di Guerra to Mrs E Huntington

From Huntington, Gordon Harold, Signalman 2575957
Campo 70 PM 3300 Italia

Written 28/7/43
Received 7/9/43

My dear Mother. Are you worrying about me? Please don't dear – I am quite all right and can take care of myself. I am confident that I can stand anything now except the thought that you might not be well. So please write to reassure me that everything is lovely in the garden, and that you are as cheerful as ever. Your son Gordon.

Posta di prigioniero di Guerra to Mrs E Huntington

From Huntington, Gordon Harold, Signalman 2575957
Campo 70 PM 3300 Italia

Written 18/8/43
Received 20/9/43

My dear Mother. I am so glad to hear you are quite well and cheerful. Don't worry dear, everything will finish up all right in the end. I wonder how many letters you have had from me by now? I have had 54 altogether from people at home, mostly from you & Dad, and Edna. One from Grandpa, 2 Betty, 1 Auntie Maud, 1 Bill Andrews. The parcels have now gone back to one in ten days from the Red X and we rather feel the difference, but who cares as long as the war will be over soon? I have had no personal parcels yet but they should be getting here soon – some chaps seem to get quite a lot but they have been in Italy longer. Cigarettes and chocolate are now the main thing – cigarettes being a form of currency as they have been ever since last June!

In spite of all, I am older and wiser for my little trip abroad and I have only one regret. That is that I am out of it. I do like to be doing something you know – I hate idleness really. Just you watch me after the war... I shall be a terror for work! Give my love to Douglas and Dad, and wish Ken all the best from me. I have also written to Dad along with this letter. Take care dear. Gordon.

Posta di prigioniero di Guerra to H Huntington Esq

From Signalman Huntington G. H. 2575957
POW Rest Camp

Written 18/8/43
Received 20/9/43

Dear Dad. I have had two letters from you recently, redirected from "Campo 85" and I was surprised to hear in one that Ken is going abroad. I do hope he will be all right – I wish I were with him though. Please let me have his address as soon as you get his first letter, and I will write to him. Meanwhile I must hope that nothing further will be asked of No. 23 in the military department! Wish him the best of luck from me...

I am glad to hear that Mother is being so marvellous about it all. You know – I follow the progress of this poultry very closely be cause I think it is a good thing to be able to pick eggs up in one's own back-garden, don't you?

Dad, I want you to find out about my income tax. I wrote to you previously about this from the desert but you may not have received the letter. I don't want to be "stung" for a few thousand when the war is over, so can you find out the position from the Prudential? Or would you advise a complete silence?

Many thanks for the books you are sending – I am looking forward to a little study. So far no parcels received from home – just now cigarettes and chocolate of great importance to me, so here's hoping! All my love to you. Gordon.

Posta di prigioniero di Guerra to D. W. Huntington

From Huntington, Gordon Harold, Signalman 2575957
Campo 70 PM 3300 Italia

Written 25/8/43

Dear Douglas I had a letter from Mother and one from Kenneth yesterday. I wish you all the best of luck in your Matriculation: what plans have you for the future? Mother tells me of the radiogram. I wonder what records you have got. Have you "Invitation to the Waltz", "Dance of the Hours" or Tchaikovsky's (?) "Nutcracker Suite"? I should like to hear from you if you can write to me at any time: it is so long since I last saw you all.

If you should be going into business Douglas, choose exactly what you wish to do, and do it. No matter if at first your choice does not bear fruit, it will eventually.

I find at the moment that time drags a little because I have not yet received a book parcel, and the books I want to read are difficult to get hold of. It is too hot for football – indeed the weather is perfect for those who are free. All about us are the Apennines, green and gentle, and the fruit trees are many-coloured. I hope to go for a walk tonight, of course under guard! Well once again all the best of luck Douglas; give my love to Mother & Dad. G.

Poste Italiane Cartolina Postale Per Prigionieri Di Guerra

From Huntington, Gordon Harold, Signalman 2575957
Campo 70 PM 3300 Italia

Written 25/8/43
Received 22/9/43

Dear Dad, I am not able to write to you as much as I want to but no doubt you understand. Your letters are fairly regular; much to my delight my total mail amounts to 60 letters to date. Glad to hear all well – I have written to Ken to wish him luck. How is business? All my love to you at home. G.

Reference: - 3063   Tel.: Kensington 6466

ROYAL SIGNALS ASSOCIATION, 44 PRINCES GARDENS, EXHIBITION ROAD, LONDON S.W.7.

12 November 43

Dear Mr Huntington,

We were all delighted to hear your good news when Mrs Huntington telephoned and we are very happy on your behalf.

Thank you so much for returning the coupons so promptly. This is a great help to us in keeping our books straight and we wish every one behaved as well! It is rather disappointing that he received no parcels during his time in captivity but we can wish him nothing better than that he will soon be home with you. We would warmly welcome a visit from him as first hand news of life in Italy would be most interesting and we would be so glad of any suggestions he may have as to anything we might be able to do for our men who have been moved to Germany.

Yours truly,

Anne Clementi Smith
Hon. Secretary

Air mail letter to Mrs H. Huntington.

From Signalman Huntington G.H.
2575957
3 P.O.W. Rest Camp

22/11/43

Dear Mother,

I wonder whether you have received any notification that I am free yet? And on my way home.… isn't it marvellous? I hope to be back for Xmas and the New Year dear – this Xmas 1943 I mean! But don't bank too much on it – we have had several disappointments lately, and sometimes we think the Army has forgotten us. We have done our side of the bargain – that is, escaping. We now wait for them to do theirs.

Just now I am having a nice comfortable time in a rest camp. We could not wish for a better place as regards food, cigarettes, etc. – but the annoying thing is that for two nights I slept in soaking wet blankets here – a thing that never happened when I was behind enemy lines even, so I am wondering just what does go on in higher, and no doubt dryer, circles when escaped P.O.W.'s are allowed to jeopardise their already diminished health by sleeping in damp tents.

Well dear give my love to Dad and Douglas – and don't worry any more. I can look after myself, you know that, don't you? Where is Ken now? Tell Edna I am longing to tell her heaps of things.

Take care,

Your son Gordon

Card from POW Reception Camp to Mrs H. Huntington.

Card from Reception Camp No. I POW Reception Camp On His Majesty's Service

Written 10/12/43
Post Mark Liverpool 11/12/43

I have arrived here.

I am well.

No visits allowed but I hope to be with you in a few days.

I will telegraph as soon as possible

Signature *Gordon Huntington*

Telegram sent to me from my aunt (my father's sister) Doris Spurway (née Huntington) in Sydney, Australia.

CABLE AND WIRELESS TELEGRAM LIMITED
"Via Imperial"

LC HUNTINGTON 23 CRICHTON AVE WALLINGTON SURREY OVERJOYED NEWS GORDON SPECIAL GREETINGS LOVE SPURWAY 23

THE EVENING NEWS
LONDON, THURSDAY, DECEMBER 23, 1943

THIRD TIME LUCKY

After two months tramp in the mountains following escape from an Italian prison camp, Signalman Gordon Huntington, of Crichton-avenue, Wallington, reached the Allied lines and has now arrived home for Christmas. Two previous efforts to escape failed.

A somewhat garbled and misguided newspaper report of the escape.

WALLINGTON & CARSHALTON HERALD

THE WALLINGTON AND DISTRICT EDITION OF THE "HERALD" SERIES OF SURREY NEWSPAPERS
FRIDAY, DECEMBER 31, 1943

The Third Time was Lucky

Signaller Huntington Escapes with a Price on His Head

Third time lucky came true for Sig. Gordon H. Huntington of 23, Crichton-avenue, Wallington, who, a prisoner of war since June 20th, 1942, failed twice in attempts to elude his captors, but on September 12th of this year, while in captivity at camp P.G. 70 (Fermo), Italy, he and 262 fellow prisoners, watched by the Italian guards, whose country had surrendered but a few hours previous, cut through the barbed wire defences and disappeared into the surrounding mountains to begin their perilous trek for freedom.

"We had been told not to move," Sig. Huntington said, "as the British were expected to take over shortly, but many of us wouldn't wait, so we escaped. We were scarcely away from the camp, I and a South African captain were in the hills overlooking the prison, when we saw the relieving party take over, but they weren't British. The Germans had got in first and numerous patiently waiting prisoners lost their chance of freedom.

"With a reward offered for our capture, and evading the Fascists, we made our way towards the allied lines, travelling mostly by night, sheltering in the homes of the Italian peasants who fed us and kept us alive. We had many narrow escapes from our hunters, but even tually, worn out, with our clothes literally in rags, and after nearly two months of plodding over rough ground, hills and mountains, we contacted the Eighth Army in the Termoli sector of the front."

CHRISTMAS RE-UNION

Sig. Huntington who left his South African colleague when they both parted to return home, arrived in Wallington on Monday, 13th December, just in time for a grand Christmas family re-union.

Gordon Huntington, who is the elder son of Mr and Mrs H. Huntington, was educated at the Wallington County School and before joining the territorials in 1938 he was employed in a London branch of the Prudential Insurance. He went to North Africa in 1941 and after serving for barely a month was captured at the fall of Tobruk. In the early stage of the journey back to Benghazi he tried to slip the lines and escape but was spotted and had he not immediately returned might have been a victim of the guards rifles. When he arrived at Benghazi he again attempted to escape but when hiding under an army lorry he was discovered.

After a roundabout passage via Greece he was sent to Italy where he was moved from Taranto to Brindisi and then later to Fermo.

"Reading and sport were the main activities of our prison life," Sig. Huntington said, "and as we cooked our own food (the equivalent ration of the Italian soldiers) we could never grumble at that."

Mr and Mrs Huntington who were surprised to see their son looking so well after his many experiences were delighted to have him back in time for Christmas.

ROYAL CREST

By the KING'S Order the name of
Signalman G.H.Huntington,
Royal Corps of Signals,
was published in the London Gazette on
15 June, 1944,
as mentioned in a Despatch for distinguished service.
I am charged to record
His Majesty's high appreciation.

Signature
Secretary of State for War

WAR OFFICE

WAR OFFICE CREST

P. 343571   22 June 1946

Sir,

    Now that the time has come for your release from active military duty, I am commanded by the Army Council to express to you their thanks for the valuable services which you have rendered in the service of your country at a time of grave national emergency.

    At the end of the emergency you will relinquish your commission, and at that time a notification will appear in the London Gazette (Supplement), granting you also the honorary rank of Lieutenant. Meanwhile, you have permission to use that rank with effect from the date of your release.

                       I am, Sir,

                       Your obedient Servant,

                       Signature

Lieutenant G.H. Huntington
The Queens Royal Regiment

Letter I received from Phoebe Waters (Pat Water's sister).

HAMPSTEAD,12, AKENSIDE ROAD,
7891 HAMPSTEAD,
LONDON, N.W.3.

27th June 1957

Dear Gordon,

By this time I'm sure you must be wondering what had happened to Pat.

The fact of the matter is that after having a wonderful time on the Continent they returned thinking that they would spend a few days with us & then go to Scotland & see the rest of England. A few days after their return, however, they received a letter from the woman who was looking after their two youngest sons, intimating that they were becoming somewhat of a burden. The result was that Pat immediately started making arrangements to return to S Africa earlier and in fact they managed to leave almost a month before they had planned to. It was all very sad and disappointing.

I'm enclosing some photos Pat took in Italy — he has given you the details on the back of each one. He would have sent them to you direct, but had apparently not taken your full address. All he had was 17 Purley Hill, Surrey. I see though you had given your full address on the back of your photograph.

Pat asked me to tell you that Mama Illuminato sent you her very best love.

I don't know whether you've got Pat's address in S Africa, but here it is in case you haven't:-

A.P.C. van den Heever,
Michele,
WAKEFIELD ROAD
RONDEBOSCH – CAPE TOWN.

Pat also asked me to tell you that he hopes to see you in South Africa one of these days.

I can't remember when your wife's babe was due. I do hope all goes well & that you are happily settled in your new home.

Kindest regards to you both.
Phoebe Waters

Chapter 13:

Home at last!

I had been thinking on the voyage to Liverpool how unlucky it would be to get torpedoed on the last lap, but here we were. Home!

I had remembered my friends in transit: Sargent Gerardi, young Oscali Cisbani, who left in tears at our last farewell, Luigi, his uncle, and other relatives who had followed with robust hospitality and I could only think of one word: Sympatico! Their word. I cannot put a meaning to it, but basically it amounts to – you like people whatever language and colour – and they like you! Italians seem to have a copyright in this word. I found them very lovable people and it seemed to change my life from then on. Pat went out there later, after the war and visited the Illuminati family, Mama Maria, Santina, Milena and Reggio.

In particular, recalling Oscali's tears and affection at our parting, he was thorough in his love and help by ensuring that we met all his family in the general area around Fermo. The night of the "Fascisti" stood out. During the time we were there they made me feel one of the family. His aunt had even sewn two buttons on my shirt and mended one sock! All this had taken place over a period of only about twenty days!

I said, "au revoir" to Jim, who had been a sturdy friend throughout, and reached home rather tired. I had been away for eighteen months and I felt very strange and self-conscious walking up our road – but I knew that at the end was my family and lovely Edna, my fiancée.

In moments like this, I ponder happily upon such questions as "What have I learnt since the big moment in September

1939?" And "What benefits and difficulties have been across my path?" I had wonderful loving parents, and a good solid family built around it. My expected career would have been a sober one, in agreeable surroundings, with reasonable reward, and an assured retirement after building a family of my own. This would have acquired its own behaviours, hobbies and a circle of loyal friends.

Dad had taught me all the sports outlets from age five. Among them football, cricket, indoor and outdoor tennis and bowls. Also, billiards, chess and bridge but – most of all – manners and the love of books. Now that seems a pretty good start – to use litotes to its full! He, obviously, like Mother, did not like too much my joining the Territorials in 1938, but they certainly understood it, as did thousands of other people.

Well, I certainly was a different person from the 1938 chappie! Hardened, wary, wiser and in love. Again, I pause to consider what I have learnt new about life, and its many facets and suppositions and I wonder how we have achieved any "abilities" and whence they have derived. Is it a legacy from our family trees?

Going back to my grandparents, Dad's side first, there was only a grandfather. William Huntington married Emma Maria Simonds and they had four children. Unfortunately, Emma died aged 43. William was very strict, very learned and had to have help at home then. He later met the daughter of a knighted gentleman. She was called Maud and they married. She fitted the part wonderfully until just before he died aged 100! He had been good at sport and charming with the ladies (as I could tell by the number who attended his funeral). I organised his funeral as well as Maud's as my own Dad was not well enough on either occasion.

On my Mother's side, Grannie (née Anne Mensley), who had always been a friend to me when I was a young child, died at 93 – her husband, Albert Pollock, had died at 81, and he had made, and lost, a fortune before that by going out to Australia gold-seeking. She had followed, by boat, all alone, in 1870 to fetch him back, knowing him well and loving him too. They then

William Huntington, Gordon's grandfather, Director & Secretary,
Norwood Institute. Taken approximately 1894.

had a good house in Streatham, not far from Gleneagle Road, Streatham Hill, where I was born. They also had another house on the Brighton seafront and two Rolls Royce cars until just before the Russian Revolution, before World War One. Unfortunately, he had too many Russian shares and they became valueless. My young Aunt Hilda kept them until the end – always hoping – but, no, they never became worth anything. He was a dear, jolly man whose visits I adored. He was an oom-pah-pah! singer (in dubious keys) and a one-finger pianist! Never mind! "When is Grandpa coming, Dad?" I used to ask. He retired with only a puny pension which was a great shame.

I must admit that I tend to believe that family life is all-important. Those who have not come under its usually kind premise, are not normally the fortunate recipients of a decent upbringing, with good manners a main item. Of course, it does not follow necessarily and families do have clashes when they live in small houses. By and large, though, I contend that family life of the right sort has helped a great deal to win two horrific wars! So we ought to get back to it pretty soon!

The Americans, in their infinite kindness, have tended to introduce "Call me Charlie" to schooling and "We're all good buddies" to their children. When it comes to formalities, they overdo it to an infinite degree. There's not enough balance to that way, although only good is intended. When babies are expected, premature provision is not the best way to plan this wonderful event, and I do not think it is always a good thing to have predictions presumed. Life is not that straightforward anyway! Life is hard and the sooner one is aware of this, the better!!

There was a particular incident when the differences between American and British culture stood out for me. When I was about seven, I read Comic Cuts, paid for out of my pocket money, and Dad was looking over my shoulder, without my knowing and Felix the Cat was being kicked out hard. "Get out you what?" came from Dad. "Get out you Bum? You'll not be reading that for a while". Dad was furious. I am reminded of this episode every time I hear an American use the word. Their "Bum" is a no-good waster. Plenty about?

I had had little news from home for a long time, in fact eighteen months, barring a very occasional letter from Edna which managed to squeeze through. I had won a lottery for a free letter home, by a stroke of fortune, and had shared it with Cecil Fischel, giving my Dad his address in Southport. I heard later that my Dad wrote to Cecil's parents and they were grateful to hear he was alright. My Dad had then told Mother that I was okay! He had kept the fact that I was a prisoner of war to himself all that time to save her feelings – amazing thoughtfulness! But he was like that in so many ways.

I was movingly greeted by my parents and I really was reticent for a while myself. I rang Edna and she was very emotional. I went round to her home that evening and met one or two neighbours on the way round. I felt strangely awkward when we went for a walk – it had been so long since having her anywhere near me, that I seemed to have forgotten my lines, and for me that was not usual! At 24, too! Well I had six weeks leave now to get it right, I thought. As it turned out, it was the same between us the next day. It was as if we had never been apart.

Edna was her bright and pretty self and she seemed just as before when I called round a few days later and I said, "Shall we go somewhere special tonight?" "Oh, no I can't, I'm afraid," she said, "I've got a date!" "What?" "I'm sorry. I've had it arranged before you came home". She told me blushingly that she and Ruth, her best friend, had a job helping in the Forces Canteen at Croydon Airport and they had met some people. "What people?" I asked heatedly. "Canadian Army chaps. It's nothing serious, Gordon", she added, "I'm sorry". "I think you had better give me my ring back. I'm sorry, too". "No – I won't give it back!!" and that was that..... on the way out I called into the kitchen, "Goodbye, Mrs Clark" and went out, fuming. Thus began the unhappiest six weeks of my life. Wow! And gor blimey too.

I didn't have exactly a diary of appointments just yet, but I had some money from Mother who had received certain pay from the Army by arrangement. As well as this I had my pay from the Pru. Dad had managed, at great lengths, to have this increased by £10 a year to £80, when he established that I had achieved Matriculation in 1936 and not been rewarded for this by the Pru. There was a thick pack of letters he had exchanged with my old Headmaster and the Prudential to prove his valiant deed! What a man! And what patience!

Not long after I had arrived home amidst lots of joy, my father handed me a letter addressed from Algiers. His face was solemn as he said that he had opened it when it came the week before; he apologised with his usual "politesse". "But this cannot be good for you, Gordon. I only skimmed it, though". It was a letter from Charmaine who had been one of the girls that my friend, Ray, and I had taken to see "Laurel & Hardy". They were the Free French privates who had wanted company in Algiers. But in the letter, Charmaine said she had fallen in love with me and would like to continue the friendship. I explained this to Dad and said I didn't intend to maintain the relationship – it meant nothing to me. Then, of course, followed the break-up. Ouch! Yes, sir!

I had to have a plan now that Edna and I had parted so suddenly. There had been no time at all to think properly, in actual fact, since I had got home with all the emphasis of the drama of rehabilitation and the joy of reuniting with my parents and Douglas and Ken, my brothers.

I started to miss Edna right away, as I was now on leave for all this time of six weeks with no companion, let alone a fiancée! She had mentioned certain events to give me clues as to her whereabouts in her spare time, so I set about furtively visiting the airport canteen, and a dance hall in Croydon, plus anywhere else I could think of like that. I played a great many records of mine at home for solace, but they made me more morbid. I checked around with local people to find out who might be at home on leave as well.

Mary White, my ex-tennis partner and rather beautiful as well as a cracking good player, was reported to be at home. I knew her mother, who was a widow with a nice house and a clothing shop in the vicinity, and called her up on the phone. Yes, Mary was at home, and came to the telephone. Yes, she'd love to see me! So I took her to the Locarno in Streatham a couple of times. I also tried and succeeded to get other dates with other girls during the weeks remaining of my leave, which disappeared quickly it seemed.

I had to report to a barracks in Croydon at the end of it. I was given a thorough test there, something in the way of an I.Q. matter and told to wait a day or two to get an instruction, which came soon, and it was to report to a place in Derbyshire for further testing. At Derbyshire, after a very strong three-day course, I was told that I had done well, but needed to be refreshed after my POW experience. So, I was sent to the Signals HQ at Catterick again!

This time it was to a recruitment company, all of them being young, with a good sergeant who was an especially efficient officer. I was put in quarters of about twelve in a room. The course was in the process of starting and I certainly was refreshed after all that time off.

A few days after it started, there was a message over the announcer, "Will Signalman Huntington please go to the Company Office and read the Orders at once." Which I did and to my amazement I had been mentioned in Dispatches "in the London Gazette" and to be properly dressed as a consequence as soon as possible! A Scots girl in the office came out and congratulated me sweetly. She was pretty and charming and added, "Hope to see you again soon. My name's Jenny". I gave her mine and went back to school again a happy man!

I began to feel rather self-conscious for a while. The RSM put me straight on where the small decoration had to be put. Our officer asked me if I would take the class for a lesson on my experiences and I paused, thought, then said, "Delighted, sir". Which I did, and got a lot of interest and questions. Thereafter, there was a different atmosphere in the camp, so to speak, and we got some football going in the unit. They asked me if I would relay-race for the regiment, when they saw I could run quite fast. I was pleased to be so fit!

Shortly after that I got a letter in familiar writing and I could not open it fast enough in my excitement. In this letter, Edna told me that she had missed me a lot. It was all happening! I was ordered to see the Colonel who said that he should recommend me for a commission and would if I could take infantry instead of Signals. I said again, "Delighted, sir".

I replied to Edna in like spirit and she wrote and said that she was coming up for three days to stay at the Catterick Hotel, right by the racetrack, not to bet, but to see me and have a real chat. This was significant and proved to be a renewal of our vows to get married soon. Yippee! My officer was at the same hotel, dining with others and saw us together. I had forgotten I had promised to go to a dance with Jenny and asked one of my new friends to stand in for me. He was a Scot, too... and he did...

Both Edna and I thought that we could marry up there in Richmond, Yorkshire, which was a marvellous village near the barracks and had a lovely church and some interesting pubs. I went to see the vicar and arranged for banns to be called. It didn't stop there, however, as Mother and Dad and Mrs Clark, after some discussion, all thought it should be celebrated at home at St Mary's, Beddington Park, Surrey. And so the wedding location was changed.

I enquired about leave and they gave me a week which was very good news. We fixed up a honeymoon hotel at Keswick Station and some digs near the Signals for later. I got my "best man" at the last moment – my school captain Ken Baker, bless his cotton socks! I travelled all night back to Surrey on the day before the wedding and quickly washed and shaved at home before going before the vicar and we became man and wife! Quick enough!

Needing to catch the train back to Keswick, we had no chance for a party ourselves and went straight to the Station Hotel which was very comfortable. But you would never have thought there was a war on! It was a good old country type pub and we were welcomed with broad Cumberland humour! It was a memorable two days. The honeymoon was a joy in spite of almost perpetual rain, but we had lots of laughs and it's a beautiful area at any time. Edna was wonderful. We took a train back to Catterick and stopped the night in a house already booked previously.

Gordon and Edna Huntington, just married, outside St Mary's Church, Beddington Park.

Gordon and Edna Huntington, on their "second honeymoon" in Torquay in 1944.

On arrival at the barracks next day, I received a letter from a lodgings in Richmond that I had previously approached, saying that we could have two rooms at the top of a very nice house for as long as we wanted. What luck! It was right in the centre of the village and owned by the taxi man, who took Edna there when she had the three days visit before.

Whilst Edna and I were in Richmond, there was a horse called Dante which was training nearby. It was 8-1 to win the Derby, so I put £20 on it. Just like that! Its form had been good and it was 2nd in the 2,000 Guineas in March. I had certain savings and considered it a very good price indeed. And it won at 1½ lengths "going away" in May. Far be it that I would encourage young marrieds to gamble as a habit, but sometimes it pays to back your convictions. In any case, Edna had secured a part time job in the bank at the Richmond branch of the National & Provincial where they badly needed someone trained to fill a vacancy. One day she overheard certain words when one of the trainer's staff came in. She knew nothing about horses, of course! But it helped….

There followed a very happy period. We had lots of fun with some of my new friends at "Signals", as we affectionately called the corps, enjoying our company. Shortly after that I had to go on a course of pre-officer training (Pre.OCTU) at Thirsk. There followed the OCTU training – a long course into the wartime "Sandhurst" at Aldershot, Hants. Successful completion of this course meant progression from a cadet to an officer. I emerged a fully blown second lieutenant.

Edna went home to her mother then. I had been told by the RSM at Thirsk that there was a special reason for that course and when we had become officers it transpired that the pass-out parade was to be attended by the King and Queen! The only difference was that there were no horses going up steps as there used to be in pre-war days. It was a thrilling experience indeed – and one to make me proud. It was a Coldstream Guards parade also.

I made several friends at OCTU, including Jimmy Dawson and Ian Hunter-Blair. I took the latter home, to Edna's home, one afternoon and he met her mother. I mention him in particular,

No. 18 Platoon "D" Coy O.C.T.U. Aldershot December 1944. Gordon Huntington second from left on back row.

as he was my partner on a scheme and he was reprimanded unfairly by the officer in charge. I had to speak up for him and got a telling off. It was all to do with live ammunition being used in the pass-out scheme on Snowdon in North Wales. I had to go before an enquiry next day and thought I might lose my commission as the result. But I was saved by giving the chap an apology and they said my record helped!

I chose the Queen's Regiment as a preference and was allotted to it. My next station was Maidstone Barracks and I was given a platoon of my own right away and met the officers at dinner in the club, which was paid for by all of us. Ouch! The Colonel was a sporting type which suited me and they welcomed us very cheerfully. The Colonel liked punctuality and got us all involved in many "rugger" matches (in full uniform!) in the mess and I seemed to excel there!

I won the doubles tennis with Ian Buckland who had been a POW in Germany for four years. I was appointed Sports Officer as an additional duty, much to my enjoyment – then Weapons Officer as my promotion to Lieutenant came along.

Edna and I found a flat in Maidstone very conveniently – we now had a baby son, Richard. He was very good at nights as a rule, so we often fixed bridge with three friends, Ian, Brian and André who remained in touch with us for years later.

I had to instruct newcomers on weapons – this time the correct ammo was supplied live for the Bren guns! My sergeant was very helpful, especially when the war was over and we had to defuse two quarries left with live bombs locally. We had used them a great deal and the job went on for several weeks. His name was Len Dally; again he became a friend after 1945.

Whilst at the Barracks I passed my full Driver's Licence including Heavy Duty Vehicles and motorcycles. We did, in fact, also win the Sports Prize in the Divisional contest after the main tournament. In addition to this, I carried on a circle of car sales in Maidstone as a sideline for our savings.

When we were demobbed, we stayed at my folk's home for a while but at last Dad had to say that we should look elsewhere. Quite by chance we were offered two rooms by John Hebblethwaite's mother. She had a house in Wallington, Surrey with her husband, a baker and John was a pre-war friend.

This move turned out to be a significant step forward in our lives, although we were not aware of it at the time. It was a nice 1920 house in a good road and comfortable. Living opposite were the Robinsons. David Robinson had attended Edna's primary school. And they were bridge fans!

Gordon Huntington's Medals:
The George VI 1939 – 1945 Star
The George VI Africa Star
The George VI Italy Star
The George VI Defence Medal
The George VI 1939 –1945 Medal, incorporating the oak leaf to
indicate a Mention in Despatches
The George VI Territorial Army medal For Efficient Service.

Chapter 14:

Back to the Pru

I did not know how I was going to be received when I went back to my Pru job at Whitechapel. It had been six years. I had been an officer, spoke in a rather more gentlemanly way, it would seem, so my cockney inheritance had been sacrificed. When I turned up at the office to report, I was clad in a new suit, black Homburg hat, at which Dad had said quietly, "Quite a smart hat, I see", and in I went.

Hardly anything had changed! Or anybody, but there were more typists – it was a District office after all. And these people had all been at the centre of the air raids. Regularly! They were all very cheerful, and welcomed me warmly but I don't think they knew quite what to do with me. Downstairs in the public part the Chief Clerk, who had trained me as a wicket keeper for the cricket club, said they would get me settled all right. "Do you still have a flutter, Huntington?" he teased! But after a few pleasant weeks I went to the Divisional Chief, who had asked me for a winner in 1938, and said that I should like to become an agent, calling on houses to sell insurance. He was absolutely delighted, so I got an agency promised in West Norwood, not far from our home. A bus ride in fact.

We now owned the house that Mrs Hebblethwaite, my friend John's mother, had owned. They had confided to me that they had an option to buy it as tenants, but her husband had a place in Surrey – a bakery – to go to. So I had suggested that, if I paid the costs of purchase for them, I would arrange for their option to go to me and Edna all in one deal. They agreed readily to help us. I had found an old gentleman in Bishopsgate with "Windsor

& Brown" as his business name. "I've never heard of it before" he had said, "But I'll try it". And he did and it worked. The price was very low - £1,000 or so. Usually the Pru liked agents to live in their agency area, but this was quite near and it was a pleasant house with a garden and chickens!

The Superintendent of the West Norwood office was a very efficient man and he said I would have a lady collector for a week to show me the ropes – so off we went. She was very helpful indeed and likeable. The job was pleasant. We had weekly meetings. The collections were made on certain days and times, according to a ledger I took over. I had to balance my book every day and pay in at the meeting days. The odd penny a week type policy was still in existence and each client had collection books.

Meanwhile other things were happening to change our future dramatically. I was still in touch with the two Johns of the bridge and tennis days……. more shortly…….watch this space!

My progress as an agent proceeded quickly and I got a lot of sales on my own, including a big one to a publican. They are notably difficult, being considered a bad risk, but we got him through. Another case was where a Dad objected to my selling his eighteen-year-old son a policy but we, or I, won that too by persuading Pop to think of his future. Two sales, really!

Whilst I was collecting merrily on behalf of the Pru, there was a dinner/dance that Edna and I went to, a Prudential function for the District, and we got quite a number of nice comments from others there including one from my boss at the office in Whitechapel. I had been named in the firm's magazine for doing well in Ordinary Branch – the more expensive policies. We were very pleased as it takes a lot of time to achieve any success there and not just knocking on a door.

Meanwhile, John Hebblethwaite was getting a licence for catering – he was disabled – and it was a peripatetic one, allowing one to cater in a mobile fashion! This could be marvellous if handled properly, and also with the Olympics coming up soon it was mouth watering! John was a very charming type, especially with the ladies! The Food Inspector was a lady! So, I gave in my reluctant notice to a very kind manager at the Pru and it dazed him, after my successes.

We had baby Angela on the way, but Edna had every confidence in my progress. We were aiming at four children, I said, "so plenty of money would be needed". We bought a van second-hand and had it painted yellow with a big sandwich each side. We found a rentable house, right by Penge West Station and got to work! Everything that was needed we purchased, including white overalls and two Chef's hats, bread slicing machine and preparation tables, etc.

On opening day, we set off and parked by Adelaide House at the end of the "Bridge" (London Bridge) and near the river. John Bennett and I picked an office building each and took position in the hallway of each, in chef's get-up and with a basket each, loaded with wrapped sandwiches and rolls. Our prices were low then – e.g. 8d a round for a cheese sandwich, 4d for a cheese roll, one shilling for ham and 6d a roll, etc. Our total taken was £4 6s 10d. Not too bad for those days, and only three items not sold.

I am reminded of a story to relate on the question of vanity, bearing in mind we should all have a certain amount of self-esteem in order to sustain being positive. At the time, I came to read in the press that it was becoming a men's fashion to be bearded and rather unruly looking. I read that women were attracted by this abomination of ideas. I was very happily married indeed, so I asked Edna her opinion. She liked the beard idea and said it would tickle her chest! So, I gave it a go and I gradually, lo and behold, sprouted a healthy one, and carried on with catering. However, I did notice frequent glances from the opposite sex, whereas it had never been so before.

One day, driving the van in Streatham, I was carved up by a bus on the same route, twice. I regret to say that I then manoeuvred to get my own back – and delayed moving on then! After a minute or two, I got out and walked back to berate the driver of the bus for commencing the whole matter. The conductor got out and said, "Come on, Fred. We're late. Leave the old boy alone and let's go!" I shaved it off the very next morning in disgust. Some sort of vanity had disrobed me! It is, however, I think, always best to have a portion of self-esteem if able to.

Part of the preparation for our new venture had been listing firms in each building and delivering an informative leaflet, listing our wares. It had an inviting picture of John Hebblethwaite proffering his basket. That scheme came off very well and by six months we had four rounds of calls with a local boy handling each. We received a good deal of publicity and had a great deal of fun doing all this, but it was a long day – 5 am to 5 pm – but only on weekdays.

At certain times in our lives, we meet people casually, and in the long run, that can be of significance. One day, at the bus stop in Sydenham, Edna was waiting with Richard, aged six, and met another lady with a boy about the same age. He was going to the same school as Richard. Hazel Ring lived nearby and was married to Lindsay Ring who was a caterer (in Ring & Brymer Ltd.) and they struck up a relationship. We were invited round to drinks one Sunday and Lindsay and I talked a lot of "shop". We made friends quickly, and the friendship grew to helping each other with advice. I was a small unit, but up and coming in my line and he was big, very big. I got various orders that he wanted fulfilled and I helped him on problems of staff, etc. He came to Angela's wedding in Cleeve Prior church, opposite our house where we had the reception. He became Lord Mayor of London, (old style), and eventually Sir Lindsay Ring. A very good fellow at that! Very kind and generous and a brilliant bridge player. He was a Dulwich Old Boy like Richard, our eldest son.

Some of our customers obtained in those early days have become very large now. Some were already large, like London Brick & Commercial Union. In the process of pursuing our sandwich side, we acquired a number of restaurants in Broad St Place, Liverpool Street, London Bridge, a coffee bar and restaurant in Southampton Row plus one in Wallington, which is still operating. We had a registered office in Copthal Avenue, Stock Exchange area. But we had four children and I had had enough of catering after sixteen years, so that I took Edna's advice and gave it up in 1962.

Where to go? So far for me, it had definitely paid off in life by me taking up chances when they occurred, and they do, but can flash away so quickly and they're gone forever. Now I had a wonderful wife, four children, Richard, Angela, Robert, Jayne, a very nice house in a smart area with a modest mortgage on it at 4% interest, but no job. I had £92 a month to come from Gordon-John Ltd, our catering firm. This was to pay off, for one and a half years, the money due to me by arrangement when I left it. Hebblethwaite had already left long ago – he could not work our way at all so we had given him the Wallington restaurant for compensation. And this was after sixteen years of sheer effort. I had enjoyed it, gaining immense experience on the way. I had met a great many people and had been headhunted twice. The mortgage was found for me by Len Dally, my weapon sergeant at Maidstone. He was the Secretary of the Post Office Building Society, Epsom. Small world!

Chapter 15:

Pastures new

I started following advertised jobs and had several interviews regarding a sales job, but they weren't sufficiently promising and did not pay much. Then in the Victoria area I found "Niagara Massage" and it was not what I first of all thought, a shadowed, furtive matter. The equipment was vigorously demonstrated to me by the manager and immediately impressed me. It was commission only at 20%. I took it and, after a week of training, started a unit of my own at the Ideal Home Show, Olympia, London in March 1963. I have used their fine equipment personally almost each day since. I even noticed an "ad" the other day in "TV & Satellite" for Niagara equipment. The Show was somewhat harrowing, 10.00 am to 9.00 pm, daily except Sundays, but after the month of it, I had doubled my earnings from catering! It was pleasing to be third out of a team of twenty-four in the sales figures. We had a Niagara song that we sang at all meetings. It put a grin on every face to help seize the day. The half hour break at lunch was welcome when it came.

We had moved to Purley by 1957, where Jayne was born. Her birth I shall never forget because of the possible difficulties over the blood differences in rhesus. Now we were six, including children.

In 1963 my grandfather died aged 100 and we had been helping (or at least mostly Edna) with him and his house. Edna loved decorating and so when he died, we bid for the house and got it with family approval. We moved there for a while, but then the Niagara boss in the USA wanted a change and they offered me the Birmingham office and a sales area of all except the "Home Counties and South"! This was a big step. I had to arrange my training courses, meetings and own sales. I had a caravan converted as a showroom and used it for shows, and we began matching London's figures. In the course of which I went to the USA three times for gatherings. We had moved <u>again</u> to a pretty village called Preston Bagot, near Birmingham with a rented cottage which had two acres of land with outbuildings. So Edna had plenty to do and there was a market each week a mile or two away! It was going to lead to the next exciting move in life!

One particular significant incident in my sales experiences at Niagara was when I was at a London sales meeting just before we had to move to the Birmingham area. It was always held in a large room at the back of the shop, and we were waiting, fifteen of us, to move into the back. A lady came into the shop and no one moved to assist her. At last I did, and she needed to have her Niagara pad repaired, so I plugged it in to test and it did need attention. She gave a Derby address. I told her I was going to be made a manager quite near her and would attend to it in a week or so. She seemed delighted and I forgot it – until I got up to my new office. I then remembered, and called on her lovely house in the country, took the pad back from her and gave it to the mechanic, Jeffery King, who delivered a repaired one to her quickly. She was so grateful, was this lady, that she gave me five friends to contact who had ache troubles. I got three orders out of that, including Winston Churchill's secretary, and Lady Isobel Barnett of TV fame, who later gave me further prospects, and so on. All this blossomed from taking the opportunity when it occurred.

I used my own story a great deal when interviewing and training sales applicants. We soon had a team contending with London sales and I got six of them good enough to go to the USA for conferences, two of them ladies!

I continued to use the fitted caravan on country shows. My methods were simple. Don't promise to cure, look people in the eye, speak the truth and let your own belief be seen as genuine about the product. Be punctual, cool, calm and collected. Three Cs! I would mention also that Lady Barnett gave me the okay to quote her for any future sales. Lady Barnett was of "What's My Line?" television programme fame. By the same standards, I got Stanley Matthews (a tight bargainer) to have a handset for his pains and I was delighted to give him 5% discount! This may have helped me for later orders for Derby County F.C. and Tottenham Hotspur F.C. plus Aston Villa via Stanley Baxter, another great player. In the case of Spurs, who won the F.A. Cup that year, Niagara, they said, "Got our chief player fit for the match which contributed to our success!" That was the comment made by the very tough and popular manager, Bill Nicholson, a model for any club to copy for their own club.

Edna and the family enjoyed that lovely village and cottage so very much. Our cottage had a stream running nearby and fish could be caught at times. Angela went to Stratford-upon-Avon Grammar School and the young Robert and Jayne went to the village school, which was excellent – one hundred yards from our home. We kept chickens, turkeys, geese and a nanny goat! The latter was very troublesome but Jayne took to her and coped very ably. Particularly enjoyable was placing one's own goods on offer at the market each Friday, and restocking at the same time. We made some cheerful friends there and it was next to the best pub in the town of Henley-in-Arden. I gathered no end of good advice in there inside an hour! It was a real chance to learn country ways and views quickly and amicably for all of us, as the children were around all the time. I had found in the past that I made farmer friends by shooting rabbits when we were on holiday in Devon. Wise people, who needed to face life in adverse conditions very often.

Quite near to us lived a couple of elderly people, the Bennetts, and I met Eric Bennett over a drink one day and he enquired regarding my occupation. He was apparently an importer. Quite unexpectedly, I met him a week later, again on my way home from Birmingham, accompanied by his secretary and they were with Max Wall, the comedian, and a lady friend. I never stay long in a pub, usually a half-hour, but we had some laughs and I left. Wall was hugely witty.

The children had made friends with a neighbouring family who asked us in for tea one Sunday to their spacious home. We had begun to settle!

Chapter 16:

Start and Finnish

The cottage in Preston Bagot was a joy and I continued to compete heavily with the London office in results. I met Eric Bennett at his office one day, by appointment, in Edgbaston and he told me he had looked at my base for Niagara in Sparkbrook, Birmingham and had been amazed that I could be in such a difficult job, etc. "As it so happens, Gordon," he said, "I think I might be able to make a deal with my firm if it suits both sides". "What would that be?" And he told me it was for a big firm in Finland and his job was with dealings on behalf of the Finnish government. It entailed going there for two days at my own expense, but with all costs to them when there, to be seen by a firm called NORPE who also made refrigerators. It was the sauna side that was open to the right person and a distributorship for the UK! "Yes", I said, "I'll talk to Edna to confirm, however". Edna said, "Okay by me. I think you can do well at anything if you care to try!" She was a great inspiration to be having alongside me – and it continued for 59 years.

The time between then, at Preston Bagot, was spent in different ways – forming a little team in Gloucester, going to the USA for the attainments of four of us to meet our other top sales people, (full expenses paid), and visiting my new friends in Finland. In this period I had to play a double game with Niagara, covering up the short visits, but in the end it leaked out that something was up, as they didn't call upon me to make a sales "pitch" at the next meeting in London. So I gave in my notice, so to speak! They asked me to stay on with my newly formed local group in Gloucester, and I said, "Okay, for a while".

Visiting NORPE for the first time, when asked about my sales aims, I told them one hundred sauna sales in the first year. They said, "good", but obviously did not credit that number. Neither they, nor I, knew then that I would achieve around one hundred and fifty sauna sales per annum at my peak!

Their boss and owner, who became a very good friend of mine soon, was Reijo Mantyoja and his right-hand man, Leo Lilja. The Finns were exemplary hosts, polite and patient, very thorough in details, lovers of good food and entertainment in respectable quantities. They are a nation that excels in design of a modern style, and are fastidious over detail.

My first experience on the first day was to be taken to the immaculate Sauna Club, on the edge of the Baltic in Helsinki, to be virtually christened to its magic! As follows – I entered a large sauna, with several jolly Finns and enjoyed the alternate heat and contrast of a cold shower for fifteen to twenty minutes. Then I was challenged to enter the nearby sea. Wow! Breathtaking. Then to come out and go in again several times. I could feel it was like coming to life over and over again! Came out glowing…. Then to "the scrubbing lady". The pores having been open and shut frequently by then and the scrubbing gently was the final touch. Then put on a comfortable bed, with a glass of cold lager. I felt a new man throughout! Having had a thirty-minute rest, I joined our hosts in a giant prawn supper – and so to bed, like Samuel Pepys.

I noticed that most Finns seemed to speak English, most of them meticulously. Most shops were of good quality and the cleanliness was apparent everywhere. I must have visited that country and Lapland almost twenty times and I never had reason to change this view anywhere there. They have their own ideas, like tackling medicine from source, and strict schooling. They remain unbeaten by Russian influence, yet they are alongside! Reijo visited us many times and often telephoned just to keep in touch. I asked him why. "Gordon, you speak loud clear English but you do not shout. You are teaching me!" His family were all very nice, too.

My first presentation of NORPE was on the Ideal Home Show at Olympia 1968. This was the cue, and strong hint to finally leave Niagara, which I did with great regret.

Now, firmly in the sauna business, I feel fit to introduce it seriously to whatever readers, and their families, I am fortunate enough to embrace. One hears a lot of giggling reference to the nudity factor, the scrubbing ladies and the beating with pine leaves, but only this latter factor is not normal to family practice. English people tend towards modest reference to such matters as showing the body off to strangers, but in most European countries they think little of it. Enough of that, I think. Try a sauna yourself after a tiring day, and you will want to go out for the evening in style! Fresh!

The Ideal Home Show was a great success for us. Thirty-seven sales resulted for NORPE and we had Nordic and Rantasalmi competing on the same show for almost a month. NORPE developed, so I had three other representatives working for me that I had trained in Niagara plus my son, Richard, as a part timer and Jayne occasionally. One of the team later (1971) was Jeremy Nabarro, the son of Sir Gerald Nabarro. Sir Gerald was a Member of Parliament who was said to have attended more parliamentary sessions than any other M.P. of his time. A mighty force indeed! The show was severely hard work but it was rewarding and "follow-ups" could score and did. Nordic were best known but we had made ourselves known with a bang!

During the show there were various well-known people visiting for their own publicity and most of them strongly hinted that it might pay me to give them a special deal, or even give them a sauna, but I politely declined, even though they called me "Gordon"! I didn't blame them. If you don't ask, you don't get.

At this period we had a house move pending. On one of the following leads from our debut at Olympia, Edna had found a suitable place in Cleeve Prior, a village near Evesham, of plum tree blossom fame, and it was reasonable - £6,000, to include a field of 7 ½ acres adjoining it. So we went twice to find out more. It was dated 1540 period with no footings plus a priest hole in the chimney and a wonderful inglenook fireplace. We decided to go for it and moved as soon as possible. The owner of the lovely cottage at Preston Bagot would not sell it at any price, but we had found an ideal place for our present business and Eric Bennett found an old Co-op building in nearby Bidford-on-Avon to be our warehouse for sauna stocks and accessories. Although in poor condition, it was lockable and easy for vehicles to access.

We renamed the new abode Japonica Lodge, and Edna got cracking on all sorts of domestic improvements. We had a shower put in next to the kitchen, as outside there was a yard and backway to the road. I was putting a sauna there – outdoor type and roomy. Apart from saunas arriving from NORPE, I had a very good cabinetmaker nearby in Bidford for making our own made-to-measure orders as against fixed sizes coming in from Finland.

Meanwhile I was looking at a builder's yard together with a house, which was going cheaply in Badsey, three miles away. This went through at the right price quite speedily, the owner being a widow whose husband had died recently and suddenly.

So we now had two houses, a building yard and seven and a half acres all quite nicely together in one area and Eric Bennett's storehouse in Bidford which held his stock from which I drew and sold as we progressed. We paid for the stock from Finland on a quarterly credit basis and they rented the old Co-op shop premises. I took on my son-in-law, Nick, to make the bespoke saunas and he and his wife, our eldest daughter Angela, bought the house from us! This arrangement had possibilities but I kept contact with the other chap, to go to if and when! Nick Winter was a very efficient man for most D.I.Y. work of any sort, and he did so well that I passed the fitted workshop over to him to include one large storehouse, leaving me with the office and another large storehouse opposite. I virtually became his customer.

Chapter 17:

Success and more Famous Names

Things were getting pretty busy and we appeared on the famous children's programme Blue Peter and then again later on the BBC's coverage of the Boat Show. I had a caravan fitted out with a sauna and shower facility and later went on the Caravan Show at Earls Court. On one of these (1971), the infamous Jimmy Savile must have been creeping about, as his manager tried to get me to give him a sauna and, oh boy, what it would do for our sales!! Yeah! We had quite a few well-known people suggesting this sort of idea, including TV presenters of a more respectable sort!

A lead from the Ideal Home Show produced success of quite a different kind. When I called on the businessman at his opulent office in Princes Street, it turned out that his organisation was connected to the fur business. However, the boss, who had two brothers as partners, wanted to talk about the Health Club they owned in Surrey. It was a famous one, Grayshott Hall, and they were looking to put glass on the doors and roof of their sauna. It was a big one! I asked our cabinetmaker, Mick Golder, to call and survey for a quotation. It was just up his street and he had some ideas that appealed. I put in a price that had a few suggestions at the end of it that could be an advancement for them. They accepted and we were away! They were delighted with the result and I was given two referrals at once – one of them Grosvenor House, Park Lane – an absolutely top hotel known worldwide. The other was a relative which could not be better as they were a large Jewish family and a very nice one at that! After I had called on the hotel and seen its secretary, he offered me a membership of its Club so that I could keep an eye on the sauna, because they had had complaints on certain matters lately. I accepted readily as they had a good set-up including a swimming pool.

Then, later on, the Grayshott Hall client asked to see me privately and mentioned he had thought of making a deal with me regarding a possible takeover. I went reluctantly with my friend, Ronny Finlason, to give certain figures. He could see that we were small, though good and said that he thought he might be a poor partner for me. Very nice and polite, eh? He said his own Club, the R.A.C. (St. James), could do with a member with abilities like mine and it could be of benefit if I joined. (Waiting list three years!) "Thanks, but a long wait," I said. "I am well placed to see about that," he responded. "Thanks very much, then!" I said, thinking to myself, "Clubby, eh, what?" The R.A.C. was a lovely Club and one could stay at reasonably low prices as a member, with pool, masseur, and a specially cold plunge pool, if required. I used the Club a good deal for lunch, clients, rivals, whoever!

During an Ideal Home Show (at which we were regulars for about ten years), an Arab gentleman got talking to me and I happened to say that my wife and I were going to Cairo in ten days' time. He said, "If you look me up, we can talk business perhaps". "Yes – good idea". So I did, and left Edna at the hotel. She had tummy trouble for two days, so I went to his luxurious hotel and introduced myself. I took a sauna and shower, but the shower wasn't the usual kind…. it was the hosepipe! I had noticed a gleam in the eyes of the Arab gentleman and now realised what it had meant. The attendant got me cornered and was it Hell? A very painful (he aimed at my pelvis rather too often) time and embarrassing indeed but given in a good spirit and after all, I was the guest! In the end he ordered two sun beds from me and we had a lovely meal, too. We also went for a camel ride, after some horse riding and my camel ran away suddenly, and I did panic a little. The camel ran towards the city and the main street. After about twenty minutes, I got it under control but never again, thank you. We did enjoy the holiday and purchased some fine cotton and clothes. So all round it was excellent, especially as holidays for that area at that time were difficult to get due to the war in the Middle East.

Amongst my experiences with well-known persons, probably the most interesting was with Brian Clough. He was at the top of the pedestal at the time, having worked miracles with Nottingham Forest. So, when he had moved to Derby County, he wanted changes and he was going to get them. He rang me and said he'd like to know more about saunas. I said, "Shall I send you a booklet and details, Mr Clough?" "No," he said, "I want the real thing – you!" So, I went along. Greeting me affably, he said, pointing a finger at me hard, "I want YOU to tell ME where I could put one of these saunas and no sales nonsense!" "With the greatest of pleasure," I responded. He took me all round the club, and I waited. I gave him the advice. "Not there," he said, "There'll be a mess in the place each match". "That's what it's for, Mr Clough". "Why not nearer the changing room?" "So that they'll be clean by then and be in better shape when you give your match views, sir." "Mmm. Ok." When it came to getting the order, he bartered and suggested I had said a certain detail on its worth. I said that I had said no such thing, but with a smile. "All right, then, come and have a glass of beer!" And we had an amicable half hour, at the end of which he said that I got the order because I was obviously a lover of saunas, and had been "to the point" about it all and not vain.

Chapter 18:

Business grows and life moves on

S till on the subject of saunas, one day a prominent neighbour of ours called with his lady friend and asked if they could see our sauna. My son-in-law, Nick Winter, had installed a garden house, shower and sauna on the edge of the garden facing our seven and a half -acre field. Our installer, Tony Watcott, and his assistant, Bob Russell, had laid an underground electric cable, and connected our water supply very skilfully so it was impressive with its view. As a result, we soon got an order from Cheltenham Race Course – he was a principal – the cream and icon of National Hunt racing! More followed with other courses including Newcastle. With flat racing we had many jockeys with NORPE saunas for private use, including Willy Carson the champion and now busy on TV as a presenter and two other champions since.

Probably our most famous prize was the order from Islington Council for four saunas and sunlamps, opened by the Duke of Edinburgh, who was very informed on such matters (and privately congratulated us for the set-up). This facility at one time was known as the Michael Sobell Sports Centre. We had a good name all over the country with local councils and this crowned it. My membership at Grosvenor House had been interesting because of users including Robert Mitchum and Prime Minister Ted Heath, a keen user. Other private users included Joan Collins, David Bowie and John Barry of the John Barry Seven.

Through laxity on the part of the representative of SUNAL, a sunbed supplier from Germany, I was able to contact them, invited to Dusseldorf, and obtained their agency for the UK – the visit was of interest, as I had to persuade them that the word of a British gentleman was his bond, they accepted giving me two months of credit in the end. Very useful.

The Germans also visited me later at our house near Tewkesbury and stayed the night in a very congenial local pub – then a visit to our works in Badsey. Careful people! They had a good range of sunbeds to offer.

My membership of Surrey Cricket Club was of long standing, including some junior days, but the most interesting visit caused me to meet Boris Karloff (the Monster in Frankenstein) whom I found to be very British, mad on cricket and went to Dulwich College, as did Richard, our elder son. Karloff had been my "hero" since I was fifteen.

When it came to house hunting, my darling wife remembered how much I loved ducks! She found a house with water within the grounds, and the agent concerned took us to visit it. It was called Lower Mill Farm in the village of Kemerton. The property came with seven acres of land, including three streams, all from a larger one further up the hill. Two of the streams were near the house, one flowing under it, and another across the front of the garden. A lot of quacking went on, so clever Edna! It was absolutely beautiful with a cider orchard, woods and ample wildlife. Heaven! I said we'd take it on the spot, at full price £48,000.

It was an Easter weekend and on the Monday I rang them to say I'd like it for less. The agent said, "Mr Huntington, you would be unwise to go low - I have at least three customers dying to see it already!" So we stayed on course. It had been the home of John Moore, the writer of country tales of some fame, with a dedication memorial in Tewkesbury. We met his newly married widow, Lucile, and she and Edna became quite friendly. I loved his books, and in our eleven years there met many people similar to some of his beloved characters. We found Kemerton not only very friendly (a party was given to greet us by the vendors) but crawling with rather rich people as well, so we felt obliged to more or less furnish the house from local auctions! One of them, the Conservative Party auction, was very fruitful for us, but there were a lot more going elsewhere as well.

After the first year I was invited to be chairman of the local Conservative party and I accepted with pleasure. Mrs Thatcher had many friends in the area, so there was a great deal of enthusiasm at meetings and social gatherings. So, in a short time, the London Cockney was getting close to the Country Gent! We soon knew everyone by name in the village and it was wonderful! I was used a good deal for canvassing marginal areas.

A local farmer rented one of our fields and made cider from the orchard, and gave us one lamb a year in return. We had three barns (one a garage) so we kept chickens to keep company with the ducks including two beautiful Muscovy ducks called Huff and Puff who roosted near the waterfall, where the kingfishers nested. I made a pond at the rear of the house for further encouragement, and grew asparagus as well. Game was plentiful and deer ate the roses! I started off some watercress with a sprig I had found up the stream. I chose a special spot for its introduction, outside the kitchen in a gravelly surround. Locally, there was a theatre in Tewkesbury and Cheltenham had two, plus a tasteful variety of shops, a racetrack and good shooting and duck breeding at local farms.

Our younger daughter, Jayne, got married in style in 1983. The wedding was a lovely spectacle, pony and trap and carriage and Jayne looked stunning. We had a champagne reception at the house of about twenty-five people after it. A super day!

In 1984 I handed over the sauna business to Jayne, along with her husband as a partner, but remained as adviser for a while, so that I would have more time with Edna to relish Lower Mill and enjoy all it had to offer. I finally retired in 1985. At some point in their lives all my children, and some of their partners, have played an important role in the business I started up in 1968. Since 2002 my younger son, Robert, has been in control.

Whilst at Lower Mill, an amusing incident occurred concerning my father's cousin, Phyllis Huntington. Phyllis and her sister, Dorothy, were known in our family as "the Ilford sisters", because they lived there. We faithfully kept in touch and they were devotees of my family and, in particular, they thought the world of my grandfather, William Huntington. Phyllis and Dorothy were second cousins to me. Their father was my grandfather William's brother. When both sisters were alive, I oversaw some of their financial affairs and when Dorothy died, Phyllis often turned to me for advice. She was a regular visitor to Lower Mill and it was there that the "deckchair incident" happened. Edna and I had left Phyllis gently dozing in a deckchair in the afternoon sun one summer's day. We returned later only to find poor Phyllis stuck in the chair which had collapsed under her! She hadn't been able to get out and had been calling us for nearly an hour! Not very funny but she was smiling and unhurt.

My aunt Hilda and her husband Vandy (Henry van den Broucque) had bought a property out in Ibiza many years previously. In fact, Hilda had been out there since the 1950s when Ibiza had been a charming little place and not so well known. We used to visit them and stay in a hotel. Thus, Hilda and Vandy introduced us to Ibiza and its novelties in the 1970s. We ended up purchasing some property there to use ourselves and to embrace an income from the lettings thereby. However, as life moved on, we decided to sell the property.

Later we bought another property, a seaside finca, in Lanzarote. Lanzarote is a volcanic island with a character of its own. It was a comparative newcomer to the holiday scene, as had Ibiza been in its time. Ibiza had become more for younger people, and had strayed rather from respectability, to some extent by bad publicity, I fear. In that time we had lots of fun but towards the end, sadly, Edna harmed her back. A sunlounger gave way, perceivably causing only slight harm at the time. However, it was an injury from which much later she had hindrances and which proved very painful as she grew older. We kept the finca for some years but eventually sold it.

Lower Mill and its social side kept us with plenty of interest. I took a personal interest in the local cricket club and saw that they had some nets put in, and had fielding practice as often as possible! There was plenty of shooting available and Edna now had a great many friends.

Edna's back was giving some trouble, as was mine. I also had problems in the hip area and the local doctor said I should consider a hip operation. In catering times I had used my hip a lot with tea urns, held round the waist, to go up office lifts in the early days! Once out walking with her, she had to fetch the car to take me back to the house, only two miles back. It eventually transpired that we decided to move one day soon and decided to explore the Sidmouth area. We didn't relish leaving "a paradise" but it made sense.

Fortunately for us, we found a fabulous house in Salcombe Regis, Devon. It was called Soldier's Hill House and is still there, in all its glory. A Georgian building with beautiful, sloped gardens. Its size enabled our children and grandchildren to enjoy holidays in Devon, making the most of the wonders on offer there.

Shortly after we arrived, a resident of our village, Jill Thomson, invited us up for lunch. When we returned the compliment, she brought her daughter with her to Soldier's Hill House. This mother and daughter pair turned out to be the most positive people I have ever had the pleasure of meeting. Jill's daughter went on to become the splendid and now renowned Olympic Games horsewoman, Mary King. Mary was only twenty-two when we met her and she oozed optimism. Jill was always tremendously supportive of Mary whose hard work confirms her title. I consider myself Mary's number one fan!

We were very fond of living at Salcombe Regis. However, we gradually found that the large house and gardens were becoming too much for us. It was time to move on again.

This time we found a smaller house, rather private and with a compact garden. Bright and airy, it fulfilled our needs. It is in Budleigh Salterton, a few miles down the coast from Salcombe Regis and I live here still. Edna and I enjoyed many years in Budleigh Salterton together until, very sadly, she passed away in 2003 after a brief illness. Her ashes lie under a marble plaque in the delightful gardens of St Mary and St Peter's Church, just below Soldier's Hill House.

Epilogue

Over my long life, I have enjoyed the love and support of my family. My steady and loving relationship with Edna served as the bedrock for our children, our children's children and, hopefully, our children's children's children. The family is essential to a full and enjoyable life. The phrase, "Blood is thicker than water", is one in which I fervently believe.

Actions such as my daughter, Angela, sending me a letter without fail every week since Edna passed away have meant so much to me. These letters give me a positive fillip and have greatly added to my general confidence in later life.

I hope that this book will serve as an historical record for my family. I wish that all who read it will find enlightenment about a time of enormous importance and change in Europe and how those events affected ordinary people.

Appendices

School Project Article by Gordon's great nephew, Harry Huntington, his brother, Douglas' grandson, when aged only 11.

North Africa was essential for us to win the war. If the Germans got hold of it they would be able to cut off most of our oil supply. Consequently we would not be able to use our planes, trucks tanks or run our factories etc. Therefore it was essential to defend our position in North Africa. At the end of 1941 the British had forced Rommel (German general) to retreat, however, Rommel managed to hold out till further troops arrived and in the middle of this massive fight was my Great Uncle Gordon Huntington.

Gordon was born on 26th of May 1920 and lived in Wallington, Surrey with his parents and two Brothers, Kenneth and Douglas. He joined the Territorial Army in 1938 as a part time soldier, receiving basic training. He was automatically taken to war in 1939 as a nineteen year old. He received training as a signalman learning Morse code. Following his training he was stationed at army barracks in Kent before being posted to Tobruk, Libya, North Africa. There he fought in the desert against the German army.

In May 1942 during one particularly important Battle a German Tank from the famous Panzer division came over a sand bank behind which was Gordon. Gordon had been given some ammunition and instructions for a Bren gun. Unfortunately, well actually quite fortunately, the ammunition for it was wrong, and if as he said "I had fired, no doubt I would have been blasted". Luckily for him, instead of being shot at he was captured. Gordon felt shocked and scared but relieved not to have been killed.

Initially he was kept in several POW (prisoner of war) pens in North Africa and Benghazi. Then Gordon was transferred to

POW camps in Tuturano, and later Fermo, Italy. Gordon was not really happy to just sit back and wait for help, so he made two abortive escapes from the pens in North Africa. Then in Fermo Italy, he got information from the guards that the allied forces were further south and also on the prisoner's secret radio.

In the panic, two of them got away. Gordon and a Cold stream Guardsman. Gordon managed to avoid being captured because his limited Italian was popular with local farmers. They helped him dodge the German stations. His way home was not easy. He had to sleep out in the open and eat anything he could get his hands on. Some times he got lucky when the Italian farmers helped them out by giving him and his friend food. When he finally got to the shore line he was greeted by the allied forces and sailed home. Gordon as you might expect was very worried about his family as he had no way of finding out what they thought had happened to him. They probably thought he was dead as he'd been missing for nine months!

Gordon's only injury during the war was while diving for cover from shelling, badly grazing his knee which became sceptic, fortunately it healed.

This is what my Great uncle Gordon said about his feelings and experiences during ww2 "An experience in finding out how to survive changed my character a great deal, because life is hard and not all fun only some fun".

Gordon got a mention in dispatches although he says he doesn't know why. Being mentioned in dispatches is recognition for services during the war and was printed in the London Gazette.

After the war Gordon bought a franchise to sell lunchboxes to visitors at the 1948 Olympics. With the money he made from the Olympics he opened a restaurant in London cooking lunches. In the end he had several of these lunch restaurants. However, his wife said he was working too hard so he looked for something else.

His main and last business was a franchise selling saunas which his son Robert still runs today.

Gordon married Edna Clark, who he was engaged to, during the war. They had four children and 8 grand children. Gordon commented "and were all happy"

Copy of document from National archive recommendation for honours and awards (Army)

Description	Name	Huntington, G H
	Rank:	Signalman
	Service No:	2575957
	Regiment:	Royal Corps of Signals attached 68 Heavy Anti-Aircraft Regiment, Royal Artillery
	Theatre of Combat or Operation:	The London Omnibus List for Gallant and Distinguished Services in the Field
	Award:	Mention in Despatches
	Date of Announcement In London Gazette	15 June 1944

Date　　　　1944

Catalogue ref　WO 373/95

Dept　　　Records created or inherited by the War Office, Armed Forces, Judge
Advocate General, and related bodies

Series　　War Office and Ministry of Defence: Military Secretary's Department:
Recommendations for Honours and Awards for Gallant and
Distinguished Service (Army)

Piece　　　16 May-3 Aug 1944

Pamphlet written by Gordon Huntington explaining the nature of Sauna.

WHAT IS SAUNA?

Sauna bathing is an ideal way of relieving both mental and physical stresses. The effect of the sauna is quite immediate, tensions vanish, stiffness is eased as muscles relax, skin becomes revitalised, and there is a feeling of undisturbed tranquillity.

It is a timber lined room fitted with platforms at different levels for relaxing. The higher the level the greater the heat. It is fitted with an electric stove which keeps the temperature at between 80° and 120° C according to personal taste. Moisture in the air is absorbed by the pinewood so that the heat is a dry one and the novice bather is surprised to find that, unlike the stifling humidity of a steam bath, the sensation on entering is like lying on the beach on a perfect summer's day, enhanced by a pleasant pine aroma.

Perspiration is gradually induced and relaxation becomes paramount. After five minutes, which is quite enough for the newcomer, an exhilarating tepid or cold shower is taken, which not only cools the body but removes the waste products from the skin brought to the surface by the action of the sauna. The bather steps back in the sauna and the process is repeated again for as many times as is comfortable. When the sauna is taken regularly a higher platform is used for greater heat and the time inside the heated room lengthens to a pleasant half hour or more, when the action is able to achieve more physical good. During this time a very small quantity of water can be poured over the special periodotite stones of the stove which causes a short-lived wave of extreme heat which grips the bather, sets the skin tingling and the blood coursing through the body. However, this extra facility is purely a question of one's own personal taste. A GREAT MANY PEOPLE ARE CONTENT WITH DRY HEAT ALONE.

The sauna is completed with a cold shower or plunge which closes the pores and cools the body and the bather can momentarily step back into the sauna to dry off completely. A minimum relaxation period of 15 minutes is essential to recover from the rapid changes in temperatures, after which the bather finds a renewed feeling of energy coupled with tranquillity and a feeling of utter cleanliness.

During the relaxation period after the sauna a massage achieves a great deal, whilst the muscles are still warmed and relaxed. At such a time therapeutic massage improves the functions of the skin, quickens the flow of blood and lymph and breaks down adhesion. This helps to reduce the weight in the right places and to get rid of body acids.

FURTHER READING

Douglas Huntington *The Solway Plainsman* (1995; paperback)
Douglas Huntington *Good Relations* (http://douglashuntington.com/)

Printed in Great Britain
by Amazon